D1421030

A Collector's History of Fans

A Collector's History of Fans

Nancy Armstrong

Studio Vista

Studio Vista
Cassell & Collier Macmillan Publishers Ltd,
35 Red Lion Square, London WC1R 4SG

© Nancy Armstrong 1974
Designed by Marie-Louise Luxemburg

ISBN 0 289 70394 8

Set in 11 on 12pt Apollo
Printed by Shenval Press

Contents

To the Countess of Rosse, the owner of one
of the finest collections in the world, who
has been so generous and helpful.

Acknowledgements

Martin Battersby; Geoffrey de Bellaigue, the Lord Chamberlain's Office; Miss R. Cameron, French Embassy; Peter Coke; the Offices of the Commercial Attachés for France, Germany, Italy and Spain; *Country Life*; the Librarian at the German Institute; Mrs Holland Martin at *Country Life*; Miss Jane Hoos, the Lord Chamberlain's Office; Mrs Della Howard; Mrs Therle Hughes; Mrs Nini James; Donald King, Keeper of the Textiles Department of the Victoria and Albert Museum; Mrs Mila Lewinski; The Rev. Robert Lloyd of Chartham in Kent; Miss Masiosa Marazano of the Italian Institute; Miss Susie Mayor at Christies; A. M. Louise E. Mulder-Erkelens, Keeper of Textiles at the Rijksmuseum, Amsterdam; the Director of the Museo Nazionale del Bargello, Florence; the Director, Museum für Völkekunde, Vienna; R. Oddy at the Royal Scottish Museum in Edinburgh; Miss Isabel Santos, Director of the Bayanihan National Ballet Company of the Philippines; Miss Akido Shindo of the Japan Information Centre; Donald Simmons; Mrs Staniland at the London Museum, Kensington Palace; Ian Venture at Sotheby & Co; The Very Reverend Archimandrite Kalistrof Ware. Special thanks are due to the Countess of Rosse for permission to use illustrations of her fans; to Miss Esther Oldham for her help and fan illustrations; to Mrs Madeleine Ginsberg for her generous assistance and to the Textile and Photographic sections at the Victoria and Albert Museum.

The Fan

The Fan shall flutter in all female hands,
And various fashions learn from various lands.
For this shall elephants their ivory shed;
And polished sticks the waving engine spread.
His clouded mail the tortoise shall resign,
And round the rivet pearly circles shine.
On this shall Indians all their art employ,
And with bright colours stain the gaudy toi,
Their paint shall here in wildest fancies flow,
Their dress, their customs, their religions
    show:
So shall the British Fair their minds improve,
And on the Fan to distant climates rove.

John Gay (1685-1732)

Introduction

Are fans merely frivolous and futile, or should they be taken more seriously as manifestations of cultures and tastes? Very little has been written about fans, and as a result many lie forgotten today, abandoned in a trunk in the attic, too pretty to throw away but too little understood by the owner to exhibit and speak of with authority. Of the few books published about fans, most were written during the last few years of the nineteenth century, and then with a diffident air hardly encouraging to the collector:

'The subject, though it may seem frivolous, amply repays careful study, and will not fail to interest the reader, provided the demands on both his patience and his time are not too great. Few persons have leisure to peruse an exhaustive volume about these dainty feminine weapons, which yet, however, cannot be thoroughly treated without entering somewhat into the social and artistic history of many nations. Our manifold duties and pleasures scarcely permit us more time for attention to the fan than to the beautiful butterfly which for a moment delights us by the graceful fluttering of its painted wings.'

So wrote M. A. Flory in 1895 in *A Book about Fans*, suggesting that for all the rich background to fans, they are no more than 'dainty'

and ephemeral and only to be studied by those whose lives presented them with an abundance of spare time.

How times have changed! Today's collector does not need to be a lady of leisure to have a voracious appetite for information and historical background, and there are records dating back as early as the seventeenth century B.C. (a tomb in the Boulak Museum) showing fans in various contexts, ceremonial, social and religious.

Nor does today's collector share the views of the late nineteenth-century collectors who generally looked down their noses at anything made later than 1800. Nowadays there is absolutely no time barrier at all for collectors. People are beginning to realize that the eighteenth century does not own exclusive rights to all that is fine and are beginning to appreciate all the art forms of the last 175 years: Art Nouveau and Art Deco artefacts are openly for sale in the great International auction houses; better evaluations are being made over Chinese and Japanese nineteenth-century painting, and societies of most countries have curious fans tucked away in their ethnographical museums.

The real collector does not have to concern him – or herself – any longer with the age-old question, 'What is art? What is craft?' but can honestly look for a combination of the two.

To be drawn by a fan one has to have a feeling for work in miniature; to be magnetized by exotic materials from far-away lands which appear blown together by magic rather than worked by mortal fingers; to have an imagination which can clearly visualize the social occasions when the unspoken 'language of the fan' was an essential part of passionate feminine nonsense, and a respect for the part a fan has played in various cultures, taking in, for example, the battle-fans of Japan, the feather-mosaics of Mexico, and the punkahs of India.

Shape, size, treatment, subject-matter and materials, all guide the collector today. By studying these features of a fan it is possible to date it and to allocate its country of origin. Whatever the age, shape and type, both art and craftsmanship must jointly be the theme.

The history of fans

How did it all begin, this use of a fan? No-one really knows – except the first person on this earth who felt too hot, picked up a palmetto leaf to 'agitate the air' and cooled himself down. Today the London Worshipful Company of Fan Makers is almost totally concerned with air-conditioning units, which is as it should be, but through what a rich series of deviations the fan has travelled between that time and this!

The word 'fan' comes from the Latin *vannus*, meaning an instrument for winnowing grain. People from all over the world from the dawning of history to the present day have winnowed their grain; small farmers in many countries today still do not own shiny gargantuan machines to do it for them but quietly winnow the precious cereals as part of their normal way of life, and there are references to this important task in Greek mythology, the Bible, Shakespeare, and dry-as-dust reports to-day from the United Nations.

If grain could be winnowed by a fan then the sweating labourer could cool him- or her-self down by using one too, and this humble instrument has ended with a dozen uses, from hiding the modest blushes of a naked Roman lady in a mixed bath to providing a tiny tray at the court of Marie Antoinette.

China and Japan

All the ancient civilizations of the world have recorded the use of ceremonial fans but the Chinese and Japanese peoples have the longest continuous history of the use of personal fans. The history of the fan in China is absorbed into the mysteries of time. According to ancient lore the fan was in use during the time of Emperor Hsien Yuan (c. 2697 B.C.), but the earliest written records are of two feather fans which were offered to the Emperor Tchao-wong of the Chou Dynasty in 1052 B.C., with added descriptions that his empress carried a feather fan in her chariot for the sole purpose of keeping the wheels free from dust.

Fans were enormously important in both China and Japan, their uses carefully pro-scribed within rigid court etiquette as well as ordinary social customs and the dance. Perhaps it is as a result of this that fans in the East have always been far more open to variations in technique, material, design and use than, for instance, in fashion-conscious France. Ancient types before the sixth century A.D. were of every shape and variation on the moon, the pear and the heart; they used woods, bamboos, bast or crêpe-papers, turtle shells or silks with feather-work, the tur-quoise-coloured plumes of kingfishers or peacocks and handles of iron, gold, ivory or leather. Yet the Chinese also excelled in the making of rigid fans in precious materials. In A.D. 1176 a hundred books were compiled by an imperial commission headed by Lung

Ta-Yuan, President of the Board of Rites, amongst which was an illustrated catalogue of ancient jade; here there was an entry showing four hand-screens of white jade (the most precious of stones in Chinese eyes, based on their religious philosophies) with handles of scented amber, ornamented with encrustations, inscriptions and low-relief carvings of landscapes, etc. These were offered as a gift from the Emperor Chun-Hi of the Southern Sung Dynasty (1174-80) to his much-loved empress.

It is claimed that the Chinese were probably the first to apply a painted design, or certainly forms of calligraphic decoration, on to a fan, but it was the Japanese who invented the folding fan and devised the most ingenious forms and convenient uses for the object. As is perfectly normal in Japan there is a legend about the first folding fan back in the seventh century A.D.

It seemed that there was a man, his name now forgotten, living during the reign of Emperor Jen-ji at Tamba, near Kyoto. He happened to be married to a nagging shrew and, one night as they lay asleep, a bat flew into their room, so the woman insisted that the man should get up and get rid of it. Lazily agreeing, the man lay in bed until the bat flew too near a lamp, scorched its wings and fell to the floor. At this the man did get up as the effort of catching the bat was no longer a threat, and, as he handled the little creature, he noticed how its wings folded open and shut, and he mused over the fact that perhaps a fan might be made the same way, so that it could be folded when not in use and carried in the sleeve or pushed into the top of a boot.

The oldest forms of Japanese folding fans used to be called *komori*, which is also the word for 'bat', so there may be some truth in this ancient fable. Certainly the Japanese are a people totally in tune with every aspect of Nature around them, so they see no real hierarchy in the pecking-order of animals or Nature as a whole, and give every object

1 Fan from Mandalay c.1880. The mount is of painted silk gauze, said to represent the last king of Burma watching an open-air display; the sticks are of ivory. Victoria and Albert Museum, Crown copyright

its due respect untinged with sentimentality. A Japanese might quite easily have learnt a practical lesson from a bat.

The fan, to them, is emblematic of life itself; the rivet-end is regarded as the starting point and, as the sticks of the fan expand the leaf, so it shows the road of life widening out towards a prosperous future. They are an intensely practical race and found the folding fan easier to use, and this new fashion quickly travelled across the seas via Korea to China where, according to references dated 960, it at first 'occasioned much ridicule and laughter'. Initially folded fans were adopted by the courtesans at court, but they later became respectable as all the other ladies wanted to use them.

The Japanese differentiate through decoration and use between a closing fan and a folding fan, the closing ones being brisé (see Glossary), the folding ones having a paper leaf, both almost always being made at home rather than in over-crowded factories. For their decoration they looked to the world of Nature around them, their mythological parables or traditional symbols and emblems.

Early Europe and the Middle East

In ancient Europe and the Middle East fans started out either as crude instruments, usually intended to whisk away flies, or as large ceremonial standards. The fly-whisk would have been made of grassy reeds turned back on themselves, or feathers or hairs, of a kind that can still be seen today carried by some rulers and Paramount chiefs in Africa.

The Egyptians sophisticated these crude fans to considerable lengths. Personal fans eventually began to look like a large circle cut in half and dropped into a pre-formed

2 The Flabellum of Tournus.
This upper section shows the
carved bone étui into which the
cockade vellum fan is folded.
9th century. Bargello, Florence

3 Detail of the decoration on
the vellum mount of the Flabellum
of Tournus, showing scrolling
foliage, a bird and calligraphic
descriptions. Bargello, Florence

handle, their lengths varying with their duties, of ivory or painted woods. Handles became longer and longer as it became traditional to have a slave do the work while his master languished on his couch.

As the fan developed it became increasingly an important ceremonial instrument. Even today those simple African fly-whisks are carried as a mark of rank. The Egyptians made huge ceremonial standards to attend their rulers and their consorts, fan and umbrella in one, and correspondingly gave them functions in the elaborate panoply of state. Their history provides numerous references to ceremonial fan-bearers attending their god-kings with very long-handled fans, some of feathers and some of wood painted to look like feathers. In King Tutankhamun's tomb there were two magnificent examples. They had gold mounts with embossed and incised decorations fitted with brown and white ostrich plumes, and in one case the handle was made of gold and in the other of ebony overlaid with gold and lapis lazuli.

The office of fan-bearer became the highest in the land, often granted to a hero after some victorious battle, the investiture taking place in the presence of the king: two priests helped to robe the new fan-bearer and adorn him with his ceremonial chains of office; then he held his fan (originally a single tall ostrich plume) and his crook high in the air as a sign of his oath of fidelity to his king. From then on he attended his king in every way, in battle and in victory, on ceremonial parades and in the temples, taking turn and turn about with the other fan-holders, often sons of the king.

Ritual and religious connotations were not restricted to Egypt, but appear in most countries in which fans developed. The Greeks associated several of their gods with fans, notably Jupiter Myiodes to whom a bull was sacrificed to persuade him to whisk or fan away the flies which infested the Olympic Games. Monarchs in Assyria always had two accompanying fan-bearers (invariably eun-uchs) who were as much concerned with whisking away flies as with a cooling breeze. They developed tall standard fans in exactly the same way as the Egyptians but they covered the great flat circles with astrological and symbolic signs which were adopted as heraldic devices, the practices later spreading to Greece, then on to Rome where they matched their shields to their symbolically inscribed standard. Centuries later the Crusaders in the Holy Land were amazed at seeing the Saracens with their heraldic standards and shields and brought back the practice to Western Europe.

By Roman times fans were being used all over Asia, the Middle East, Africa and parts of southern Europe and the umbrella, the fly-flap and the fan (all rather difficult to distinguish one from another) were some of the most solemn symbols of state and religion. Fans even came into titles. The ancient kings of Burma had amongst their many titles 'Lord of the Twenty-four Umbrellas' and this was the number, too, always paraded before the emperor of China on every state occasion and even accompanied him on the hunting field. In a rare and interesting fan (fig. 1) made in the nineteenth century in Mandalay, one can see the last King of Burma watching an open-air display seated upon an ivory chair and shaded by a silk and tasselled umbrella, a lady near by wafting a gentle breeze over him with her open fan.

The practice of using fans in ceremonies has even survived into modern times. In Roman Italy there was a fly-flap, a fan half-way between a fly-whisk and a standard, made of peacock's feathers with a long handle. This was called a *musicarium* and the servant who wielded it was a *flabellifer*. Later on the Catholic Church called the sacred fan *flabellum* and to this day many a devout Catholic has seen the Pope attended by fan-bearers holding their huge standards of peacock's feathers.

The fan has also taken on symbolic meanings – in the disc-shaped *ripidia* in Christian Church ceremonials, the *chauri* waved over the head of Krishna, and the visible wafting of divine influence by the attendant angels upon the Saviour in early Christian missal-painting. Divine inspiration was not merely an acceptance in the mind, it had to be felt arriving with one's physical being or even the sound of it heard through the air, for minor miracles could happen any day.

Buddhist and Moslem

In the East its religious use has been even more widespread. People who live in or have visited India are well aware of the problems with flies and have always used the *chauries* or fly-whisks; the Jains had especially soft ones made so that they could whisk away the flies from settling on their gods without harming or destroying them – other creeds were not so benevolent; and in the Elephanta Island caves near Bombay there are bas-reliefs of Brahma and Indira with their servants armed with fly-whisks ready for use.

The varieties of materials used for these fly-whisks are legion: the bushy tail of the Himalayan yak (black or white) horse-hair or various grasses, the striped quills of larger birds, and peacock feathers. Their handles were of metal, ivory, perfumed sandal-wood and antelope horn, exotic appendages as colourful as the yak-tail *chauries* fixed upon the gold or ornamented shafts between their horses' ears, just as plumes of chivalry were always fixed on war-horses' heads in Egyptian and Persian times to sweep away the flies.

Peacocks' feathers have always been associated with gods and royalty and very high office. They are the emblems of vigilance (the ever-open eye) and have been carried for their symbolism by attendants throughout the histories of many countries, either as standards or on personal fixed fans made in disc shapes. In India they often used the breast and neck feathers to make a pattern in the centre of the disc and the tail feathers formed the border. The people were so used to

singing colours in the glaring hot sunlight that all manner of materials were used to give a colourful effect; the centre of the disc-fan might be made of plaited pith or cane painted a brilliant scarlet, with inserts made from gleaming and glistening silvery mica, slivvers of looking-glass or iridescent emerald-green beetles' wings; the handles being of painted cane or wood or even with covers embroidered with a myriad of rainbow beads. In addition to the disc, they were shaped like crescents, or even flags, and all these kinds can be seen in the Buddhist caves of Ajanta (from 100 B.C. to A.D. 800), just as the same shapes are seen in Egyptian and Assyrian sculptured reliefs, or those used by the Copts in Arabia from the third to sixth centuries and then used again during the Renaissance in Italy.

Fans of immense value were made for Persian Princes, Mogul rulers and the Maharajahs of India; a very fine one of gold in a disc-shaped set with cabochon sapphires was dedicated as an offering to the Buddha's Tooth in the Temple of the Tooth in Kandy, Ceylon (Sri Lanka).

Another set of precious regalia is that from Burma, brought to the British Museum from Mandalay in 1885, amongst which are four long-handled fans of gold, jewelled with rubies and nine other stones, their handles overlaid with gold and encrusted with gems.

It is difficult nowadays for the Western European or American collector to understand the full complexities of orthodox Eastern ceremonials unless they have lived there, but they were all part of that half-man, half-god mystique which bound the peoples together, comforted as they were with the securities of their own particular traditions and established since the beginnings of history.

The Flabellum

The flabellum, or fly-whisk used in Christian churches, stemmed from heathen rites and was adopted by the Christian faith as an entirely practical asset: to keep flies away from the vessels of the Eucharist. The early Christians were neither interested in nor sentimental about the cup that Christ used at the Last Supper. However, later Christians gave more importance to the chalice, and by about 1400 its form was standardized. The new shapes had various covers and the use of the flabellum came to an end, so it is impossible to collect ecclesiastical fans to-day. However, it is still possible to see fans used in some other religious rites.

In the Greek Church, until the present century, a deacon, at his Ordination, would receive the *hagion ripidion* (sacred fan) generally in the shape of a cherub's six-winged face; in the sacrifice of the Mass he waved it gently over the bread and wine from the time of the Offertory to the Communion.

Amongst the earliest of known flabella is the flabellum of Theodolinda, Queen of the Lombards, in Monza and the magnificent Flabellum of Tournus, preserved in the Bargello in Florence (fig. 2). It is as well to describe it here as probably other religious flabella were on the same pattern if they were not rigid and made of metal, as so many were.

Basically this flabellum consists of a long cylindrical handle (over 50 cm., 21 in.) of intricately carved bone (some sections tinted green) to whose top is attached an oblong narrow box or étui (approximately 23 cm. long and 6.5 cm. wide; 9 in × 2½ in.) from within which a pleated sheet of vellum unfolds to form a complete circle.

Between the handle and the étui is a carved boss which has helped to a certain extent in the dating of the object, for there are four carved niches carrying four standing saints, St Paul with his sword, St Philibert with his book, St Peter with his keys and Mary Magdalen holding her box of ointment. It is now thought that the figure of St Paul is an early fifteenth-century substitution for a lost figure of St Agnes; unlike the other males he is bearded but has no halo.

The leaf of the flabellum is 140 cm. long and 20 cm. wide (56 in. × 8 in.) made of painted vellum and divided into three separate zones of unequal width by gilt-framed bands of purple, with thirty-eight parallel vertical pleats again dividing the fan into sections. The decorative content shows flowering volutes and leaves, numerous small animals and human figures with no logical proportions except the amusing fact that the humans are the smallest. Scholars become animated at the phenomenon that St Peter with his keys, on both the vellum and the handle, is seen without a beard, an iconographic instance of great rarity limited in Carolingian art, it appears, to the milieu of Reims-Metz whence it was communicated in the tenth century to the School of Winchester. The complicated iconography of the vellum helps to establish that not only was the whole a work from one workshop only but that it was directly influenced by Virgil's *Eclogues*.

A most scholarly work was carried out by E. A. Eitner in 1944 on this flabellum, narrowing the period of its production to between A.D. 860-75. From the ninth century to the eighteenth it had been kept amongst the sacred curiosa of the Treasure of St Philibert (died 685) at the great Benedictine Abbey at Tournus in Burgundy, on the river Sâone, south of Chalon.

Many churches are associated with flabella such as St Riquier in Ponthieu (or Centula) which was built by Charlemagne's son-in-law Abbot Angilbert 790-99, known to have had a flabellum of silver, and another was noted in the will of Everard (died 937) the founder of the Abbey of Cisoin near Lisle.

Perhaps some of the finest liturgical fans in use today are in the Monastery of St John's, Patmos, where there are some *ripidia* of the sixteenth and seventeenth centuries which still stand, two on each occasion, on either side of the processional Cross. These are placed immediately behind the altar and are also used in processions, especially at a Pontifical Liturgy; and yet others can be seen in medieval manuscripts within their library.

Because of their associations with both

4   A very early tomb-brass,
1306, showing Sir Robert de
Septvans in Chartham Church,
near Canterbury, Kent,
exhibiting no less than eight
winnowing fans on his aillettes,
shield and surcoat. By courtesy of
the Rector, Robert Lloyd

royalty and religion fans have been adapted for cermonial dress all over the world, and also in heraldry with seals, crests and arms. Richard Cœur de Lion's second seal (1197-9) shows a fan crest; this was used after his return from captivity and was probably copied from others he had seen in the Middle East; Richard Fitz-Alan, Earl of Arundel adopted a fan seal; Humphrey de Bohun, Earl of Hereford did likewise in 1301, Edward III in 1360; and upon the effigy of Sir Geoffrey de Luttrel, c. 1304, there is a fan upon which the entire Luttrel arms are arranged. An especially interesting example can be found on a tomb at Chartham, near Canterbury in Kent. On the fourth oldest tomb-brass in England (1306) can be seen a Sir Robert de Septvans (fig. 4) displaying winnowing fans, some on his shield and ailettes and some on his surcoat. The tomb is very well-preserved and it is quite easy to see his woven straw fans with their two loops to be held as handles, the straw being taken from the grain which had been winnowed. In a manuscript in the British Museum Sir Robert's arms are given thus 'Sir robt de sevens dazur a iiij vans dor' and his fitting motto was *Dissipabo inimicos Regis mei ut paleam'* or 'The enemies of my king I will dispense like chaff'.

Most medieval fans, however, liturgical or secular, were of feathers; these are seen in the Gospel of Trèves, the Book of Kells and various inventories. The Chapel of St Faith in Old St Pauls possessed 'a muscatorium or fly-whip of peacock's feathers' in 1298 and even in a small parish church at Walderswick in Suffolk in 1493 there was an entry for four pence for a 'bessume of pekoks fethers'.

The Fan in Fashion

By the fifteenth century the liturgical fan was on the wane but the great merchant traders were on the move. The development of the Portuguese as a conquering power in the Far East dates from 1497 and the first expedition of Vasco da Gama. He made three other expeditions during the first twenty years of the sixteenth century which firmly established Portugal as a formidable trading power. Portuguese sailors extended their journeys as far as China, and from there to Japan in August 1517, returning to Europe with delightfully strange luxuries. These included the folding fan for the use of ladies.

From then on the fan was no longer reserved as an adjunct to a solemn church service, no longer used exclusively in ceremonial attendance to kings and potentates, but was for the use of women of fashion, and there it has stayed.

During the sixteenth century and half of the seventeenth fans were considered as great luxuries or jewelled toys, and both rigid and folding ones were in use. In typical Renaissance splendour they were treated individually from the rarest available materials and often garnished with precious metals and stones. It is known that feather and tuft fans had occasionally been in use during the four centuries before, made from peacock, ostrich and parakeet feathers and arranged in the natural and normal way that they grew, their handles being of carved ivory, gold or jewelled silver and hung from the girdle by a chain. Now they were to be taken up and used as a fashion accessory by the most sophisticated and advanced of women in Europe, the ladies from the great Italian city states.

These cities, lying coincidentally in the paths of returning Crusaders, hot, humid and ridden with flies in summer, were ideal for the use of a personal fan. Venice, Milan, Genoa and Sienna all were known to use slightly differing types, feather tuft ones, others with mirrors in the centre and garnished with pearls, or banner- and flag-shapes affected by the wives of rich Venetian merchants. In Venice there were generally two distinct types, heavy, colourful and elaborate ones for the wealthy matron, delicate white vellum ones edged with Venetian lace for the engaged or newly married girls – Titian painted several.

Each city was proud of its individuality, so their dress was identifiably different, so were their accessories, so were their fans. The ladies from Milan carried a rigid feather fan, bound around in five sections; ladies from Naples or Bologna preferred rigid hand-screens with Renaissance ornaments, and the fashion-conscious from Parma, Ferrara, Florence and Genoa each used subtly different shapes and materials.

Even maids in wealthy European courts could own gorgeous feather fans, so their mistresses had to go one better; some fans made for the queens of the fifteenth and sixteenth centuries cost an immense amount of money and fifteen hundred crowns was not a unique sum to pay. England's Queen Elizabeth had a great many given as New Year's gifts (some can still be seen in her portraits, see p. 36). On one occasion (1574) the Earl of Leicester gave her a New Year's present of a fan of white feathers set in a handle of gold, garnished on one side with diamonds and rubies and two 'very fair' emeralds, and on the other side more rubies and more diamonds, with a white bear (his cognizance) on each side, two pendant pearls, and, emblematic of his being bound to the Queen, 'a lion ramping with a white muzzled bear at his foot'.

On another occasion (1588) the Countess of Bath gave the queen 'a fanne of swannes down with a maze of gilene velvet, ym-broidered with seed pearles and a very small chayne of silver gilte, and in the middst a border on both sides of seed pearles, sparkes of rubyes and emerods, and thereon a monster of gold, the head and breast mother-of-pearls'.

The folding fan must have come into England from Italy via France through Catherine de Medici (1519-89) who made her first public entry into Paris as queen in 1549. Catherine brought in her retinue her per-fumers, who were the traditional makers of fans in her native country, and the type of fans she preferred can be seen in a half-length engraved portrait of the queen at the British Museum. She had feather fans, folding fans and others with mirrors in the centre in her inventories. Brantôme, the chronicler of French society at that time, reports that when her husband died Catherine put around her device an arrangement of broken fans with the feathers falling to pieces and the mirror cracked – as her sign of having abandoned the frivolities of this world. It was temporary.

Découpé fans, of intricately cut paper or vellum, came into fashion in the later six-teenth century, appearing often in painted and engraved portraits of the time. For a very long time it has been known that there were only two examples of these sixteenth-century découpé fans in existence, the one at Cluny and another in a private collection. Nowadays the one at Cluny cannot be seen but, with great generosity, Miss Esther Oldham has permitted the reproduction of the other découpé fan from her collection. It is the exact counterpart of the Cluny one except for the fact that the Cluny one is edged with a series of points; the design of the 'reticella lace' is exactly the same and so are the sticks (fig. 5).

By now most contemporary fans were the folding type, still attached to the girdle by chain or ribbon and made in the découpé style. They were so popular that they con-tinued to be made in every century, generally of vellum and later in paper, especially silver paper. Another extremely early découpé fan can be seen in fig. 6 from the Messel Collection. This, too, is Italian by origin, made during the first quarter of the eighteenth century of kid, painted with scenes within cartouches and having beautiful ivory sticks. It is very pretty, a good deal of the painting is in shades of pink against the silvery white, and the découpé work is extremely sophisticated.

When fans had been used as liturgical instruments endless time and trouble was lavished upon them to make them worthy

to inhabit the House of God; as part of the great panoply of monarchy in Europe during the fifteenth and sixteenth centuries they were created as jewelled works of art made from rare imported materials, yet when fans became fashion accessories for the masses they gradually became looked upon as adjuncts of the flirt. Parsons began to rile against these ungodly practices and lampoons were written. This accorded with the traditional suspicion with which fashion fans had always been regarded. Catherine de Medici's son, Henri III, included in his elaborate dress a vellum fan, which had won him a place in Pierre de l'Estoile's *The Isle of Hermaphrodites* (1588).

Fans now had entered into a completely new stage; they were for women; they were for fashion; they were exported from one country to another, and now they have become collectable.

The history of the fan and fly-whisk of each culture can be followed in really good ethnological museums all over the world: in the British Museum in London there are examples from Hawaii, the Gold Coast, the Andaman Islands in the Bay of Bengal, Tahiti, Tonga, Samoa, Ethiopia and the Marquesas; exhibiting every known shape from circular to kite-shaped, the heart, the inverted heart, the leaf and the shield amongst others.

In the United States there are many ethnological museums which have fine exhibits, especially of their own country. Fans were nothing new in North America—for centuries they had been in use amongst the Indian tribes. Francis Parkman in his work *La Salle and the Discovery of the Great West* describes an account of the visit of a Taensas chief on the banks of the Lower Mississippi to Le Sieur de La Salle in 1682:

'The Chief condescended to visit La Salle at the camp; a favour which he would by no means have granted, had the visitors been Indians. A master of ceremonies and six attendants preceded him, to clear the

5   Rare découpé fan c.1590, made of an early rag-paper and cut by hand in a design of reticella lace. By courtesy of Miss Esther Oldham

6   Découpé fan of kid, painted with scenes within cartouches, of late Baroque style. Ivory sticks. Probably Italian. First quarter of the 18th century. By courtesy of the Countess of Rosse, Messell Collection

path and prepare the place of meeting. When all was ready, he was seen advancing in a white robe and preceded by two men bearing white fans, while a third displayed a disc of burnished copper, doubtless to represent the Sun, his ancestor, or, as others would have it, his elder brother.'

We can here assume that these fans were made of feathers and it shows how the use of the fan in high ceremonial was universal, common to both East and West alike, their origins lost in the mists of time.

None of the fans mentioned in this chapter can be bought by a collector. They are historic, some can be seen in world museums or paintings but they cannot be bought on the open market. However, as a historical background to the fans of the past three to four centuries, they reveal fans' varieties of purposes, their great dignity, and their serious content.

Painted fans

The quality of European fans produced between the mid-seventeenth and mid-nineteenth centuries depends very much on their painted decorations, and it is mainly the subject-matter and quality of decoration on a fan that interests the modern collector. It can only be the rather wealthy who continue to collect seventeenth- and eighteenth-century fans of real quality. Too many of the finest ones which remain merely go round and round the sales rooms every few years, the same small select group buying them, just as, during the seventeenth century the owners of fans were just a relatively small, select, rich and discriminating group within each country's society.

It is generally the case that seventeenth-century fans, wherever they were made, were rather dark in tone, partly because many of them were made from brown leather or thick paper (which was scarcely white in those days). All the accent was on the leaf and the sticks were left reasonably plain. When the fan was fully extended these overlapped each other, giving a massed effect; most of the leaves took two thirds or even three quarters of the available space, the simple sticks taking the rest. This also meant that the sticks seldom took on any of the same decorations from the leaf, they were quite separate and treated separately, not married to each other with the same brilliance one sees during the eighteenth century. Fig. 7 shows a fine

example of this technique in a magnificent late eighteenth-century fan from Italy, where the carved and pierced ivory sticks (backed to simulate jasper) show medallions of ships, duplicating the painted border above. The whole fan is painted in the style of Zucci, showing 'Thetis arming Achilles' in a central vignette surrounded by sequins and further Neo-classical scenes, but it is difficult to decide which is the more important, the leaf or the sticks. To find such a marriage is the greatest prize of all.

Italy

One would imagine that in Italy, the nursery of the European folding fan, fans would have been painted by the finest artists of their time. Unhappily, Italian fans of the seventeenth century never really came up to expectation as works of art, they somehow 'missed the boat'. The painting of fans came in just as the last echoes of the High Renaissance died away, up until now they had been craft-works with a huge variety of materials, and when the fashion came into being for having them with a painted decoration it was just too late. No great artists of the sixteenth century painted any or have been recorded as having done so, and by the time painted fans were at the height of fashion during the seventeenth

century the accent on fine painters had moved gracefully away to France, the Netherlands and Spain.

The earlier Italian fans were decorated from one side right across to the other with colourful scenes from classical mythology or some composition copied from the work of a well-known artist in an equally well-known building. In fig. 8 the kid leaf is painted in water-colours by an unknown artist, and shows the *Aurora* fresco by Guido Reni in the Casino Rospigliosi in Rome.

The earlier mounts were generally of 'chicken-skin' or vellum, the paintings carried out in gouache or water-colours. Indeed, the quality of some of the earlier fan leaves from Italy were good enough, like the Japanese, never to have been mounted at all. Occasionally fine fan leaves of this period which have been mounted have been taken off their sticks again and framed; because of their undoubted quality they quite often come up for sale in auction houses. Fig. 9 shows a painting made in about 1700 in water-colours of 'Bacchus and Ariadne', copied from a sketch by Guido Reni and never mounted as a fan. Fig. 10 shows a dismounted fan leaf of around 1720 painted with 'Diana as a huntress' and showing the marks where the leaf had been folded.

As can be seen the paintings are only copies of greater artists' original compositions. There are known copies of works by Guido Romano, the Caracci, Guido Reni, Guerchino, Poussin, Claude and Charles Le Brun; two subjects which were especially chosen from the huge output of Le Brun were from his tapestry cartoons of *The Triumph of Alexander* and the *Death of Actaeon*. Fig. 12 is a variation on this theme and shows a splendid plumed head-dress.

The subjects the artists chose centred round the classics or the Bible and especial favourites were 'Bacchus and Ariadne' after the Caracci, 'Aurora' after Reni, and 'The Marriage of Cupid and Psyche' after Raphael in the Villa Farnesina in Rome (with an added

7 Italian late 18th century fan. The leaf is painted in the style of Zucci, showing 'Thetis arming Achilles' within a border of sequins, together with classical urns and a frieze of ships; the carved and pierced ivory sticks are backed to simulate jasper and show further medallions of ships. By courtesy of Christies

8 An early 18th century Italian fan; the mount of kid painted in water-colours, a copy of the Aurora *fresco by Guido Reni in the Casino Rospigliosi in Rome; the ivory sticks are Chinese. Victoria and Albert Museum, Crown copyright*

9 A very early Italian fan leaf, c.1700. Painted in water-colours, showing 'Bacchus and Ariadne', after a sketch by Guido Reni, mounted and framed. Victoria and Albert Museum, Crown copyright

Below left
10 An Italian fan leaf, c.1720. The scene shows 'Diana as a Huntress'. By courtesy of Christies

11 An 18th century Italian fan, c.1740. The mount shows a well-painted view of a harbour; the thin ivory sticks are carved, pierced, gilded and silvered; the stud is of paste. 28 cm. (11 in.). By courtesy of Christies

landscape to fill the gaps). 'Venus and Adonis' (fig. 13) was an original composition by a lesser artist, Leonardo Germo, when he was in Rome; an added interest is that the fan leaf was originally owned by Benjamin West.

Very fortunate indeed for the fortunes of various Italian states were the excavations at Herculaneum and Pompeii during the eighteenth and early nineteenth centuries.

Up until 1748, when full-scale excavations began, architects had been able to copy the exteriors of classical buildings but had absolutely no idea whatsoever about the interiors of the buildings, their decorations and their furnishings. The excavations gradually revealed all; their culture, their art, small private details of their intimate lives which looked as fresh as yesterday having been so beautifully protected from the outside air. It must have been as fascinating to watch the excavations then as to read the gossip columns today or watch live chat-shows on

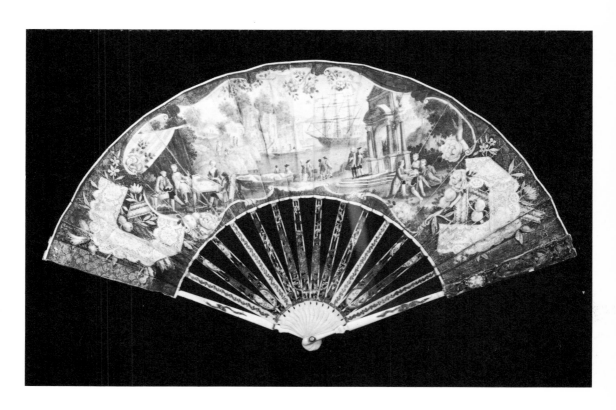

12   17th century vellum van,
Italian or French, incised
mother-of-pearl on the sticks and
guards. Style of Charles Le Brun.
Correr Museum, Venice

television, and all Europe flocked to see for themselves. In England at this time an interest in the Fine Arts was spreading like wildfire amongst the wealthy and educated. Not only was the mere acquisition of pictures and statuary becoming more valuable as a source of social prestige but it was considered desirable to possess, if not expert knowledge of, at any rate an articulate enthusiasm for the objects acquired. In fact it was not long before the Fine Arts came to be regarded as the only intellectual activity for which

enthusiasm was not only permissable but desirable.

Wealthy young men were sent on their Grand Tour, and as they travelled all over the continent, especially to visit Italy, they learned much, and they collected, to prove that they had been there; then they wrote long, enthusiastic letters back home about some (and only some) of their adventures and sent back souvenirs to the ladies of their families.

At this time the individual powers of many

13 *Italian fan, c.1700, the painted mount depicting 'Venus and Adonis' by Leonardo Germo. Victoria and Albert Museum, Crown copyright*

of the Italian states were waning and gradually they all decided to capitalize on their assets in the world of the Fine Arts, enjoying their role as centres for these rich young men and to provide gaiety, luxury and a social whirl for their more-than-welcome visitors.

Naples and Rome were delighted. Other places en route were equally pleased, for what matter where they went as long as the rich young men actually came? It was known that they came for education in the main but also that they would collect. The Italians were

quick to see how they could do well from this surge of culture-seekers. They manufactured fake antiques, they sold real ones; they created 'Greek' cameos, they were ever-ready to teach the art of drawing antique ruins. And they made hundreds of fans to take home as souvenirs. These were painted with scenes which were familiar to all of ancient buildings or cities or ports, and later on they decorated round the vignettes (when they were in fashion) with linear grotesques copied from the painted walls of the recently discovered

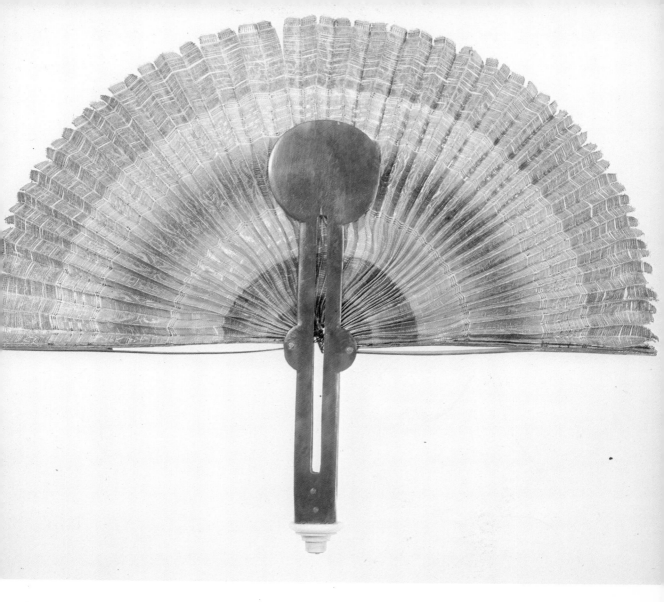

Top left
14 European fan painted in gouache on kid, showing a view of the River Tiber and Rome. Italian, third quarter of the 18th century. By courtesy of the Countess of Rosse, Messell Collection

15 Italian trompe l'oeil fan, dated 1771, signed by Francesco Stagni, painted on kid. By courtesy of the Countess of Rosse, Messell Collection

16 Fan which belonged to Mary Queen of Scots. Mount of silk and silver tissue; tortoiseshell handle from which the guards pivot, swinging round and over to enclose the mount in a case. Width 26 cm. (10¼ in.). National Museum of Antiquities of Scotland

villas of Herculaneum and Pompeii.

The Neo-classical era had arrived and all Europe was affected by the discoveries in Italy and the new styles in art. Neo-classical fans in Italy were complete little gems of public relations work which showed views of the Bay of Naples, Rome with St Peter's or the Colosseum and splendid uplifting ruins which everyone could instantly recognize. (Figs. 11 and 14.)

In Venice, too, they busily painted fans with scenes such as the Piazza San Marco (after Canaletto) or 'The Marriage of Venice with the Adriatic' (in fig. 22). Other cities naturally followed suit, painting their own views and types such as fig. 17, in which some Florentine capitalized on the foreigners' fascination with their peasants.

These later, Neo-classical fans showed the scenes as vignettes, with either one central medallion or with three, the central one being the largest with the smaller relating scenes on either side; all the available space in between had thin, aloof, linear grotesques, almost clinical in their scholarly precision, loosely copied from some newly excavated villa walls (fig. 87). Fig. 20 shows an Italian painted fan with five vignettes, the central one being the main scene.

Painters in Italy, when copying the frescoes on walls or ceilings or even easel paintings, were very meticulous in showing the exact work placed as the centre of the leaf (fig. 12). If necessary, where the leaf ended, they just chopped off the rest of the composition. In France they were more apt to juggle a painting around, making a personal composition from certain elements of some well-known painting and then framing 'their own work' with gilded scrolls or painted ribbons.

It was much the same with colours: in Italy they copied the real colours from the frescoes of Herculaneum and Pompeii – black, rust-red, pale buff and turquoise blue with much fine linear scrolling; in France they used pretty, feminine colours to match or tone with the dress, the ceramics and the general

17 An engraved fan leaf
showing 'Rustics Dancing'.
Florence. 18th century. Correr
Museum, Venice

Overleaf
18 Queen Elizabeth I, holding
a feather fan. Artist unknown.
National Portrait Gallery,
London

19 The soprano, Adelina Patti
(1843-1919) with a feather
fan by J. Sant. National Portrait
Gallery, London

20 18th century European fan.
Showing 'The Picnic' and four
extra vignettes. Encrusted
mother-of-pearl sticks. Correr
Museum, Venice

Below left
21 Early 18th century Italian
fan. Chicken-skin mount with a
drawing in sepia of 'The
Judgement of Paris' seen here,
and a classical landscape on the
reverse. Sticks and guards
mother-of-pearl, jewelled stud.
Victoria and Albert Museum,
Crown copyright

22 A well-engraved fan leaf
showing a view of Venice during
the annual celebration of the
Marriage of Venice with the
Adriatic. 18th century. Correr
Museum, Venice

air of sophisticated femininity. The background to these colours was light, and the painted decorations shaded off towards the sides into darker masses, showing groups of figures and flowers (fig. 28). Every colour in the palette joined in, especially rose-reds and daffodil yellows. Much of the painting followed the general techniques of contemporary embroidery, especially in regard to shading in a deeper tint. A marvellously shaded and tinted fan is shown in fig. 32 with its evocative scene of eighteenth-century dalliance and charming matching sticks.

One always receives, with Italian fans, the feeling of an overall painterly quality, whereas in France fans became more of a collage as snippets of this painting and snippets of that decoration were all hurled together, often with great flair and producing charming results. Erudition could be worn most lightly yet effectively, as by the unknown artist who painted fig. 26 with scenes of nymphs, satyrs, landscape and ruins. But one of the enigmas

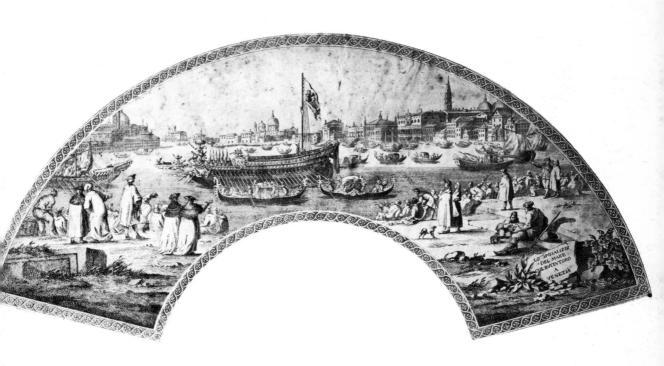

23   French painted fan from third quarter of the 18th century. By courtesy of Christies

24   Fan leaf, 'The Death of Dido', French, end of the 17th century. This is painted on vellum, probably by Gerard de Lairesses (1641-1711). Rijksmuseum, Amsterdam.

25   18th century fan showing 'The Bath'. Beautiful sticks, encrusted ivory and mother-of-pearl. Correr Museum, Venice

of painted European fans of the seventeenth and eighteenth centuries is the lack of work by the great miniaturists of the day. Was it purely because they realized that the folded lines would radiate across their compositions when they were used to a flat surface? Was it because fans were now 'dress' and not 'art'? Or was it because none of their really great and well-known predecessors were known to have painted fans? We do not know and probably never shall now; all we do know is that the minor painter attended to fans, and that the nearest they became to being major works of art were when they were copies of well-known frescoes or canvases.

Comparing the painting techniques on a Japanese fan of the same period one notices a quite startlingly different approach. There the painter, who would be an important and respected artist, considered the shape of the fan, the play of light and shade, the radiating lines which would cut across, the curve of the leaf and the colours – then he married art to craft and produced a masterpiece. European painters did not think this way at all.

In the eighteenth century it was perfectly normal to sign one's work whether one was an ébéniste, a worker in precious metals, a jeweller, a watchmaker, a miniaturist or an engraver . . . but never the painter of a fan. It is really quite pointless to look for fans painted by top-rank artists of the seventeenth or eighteenth centuries in any European country, and it is equally pointless to look for signatures. Both facts are in complete contradiction to the other established fact that so many of the decorative arts *were* signed and so many artists were painting, and signing, easel pictures.

Any fan of this period with a legible signature of a famous artist (especially Italian) is suspect – many a nineteenth-century owner, convinced that his or her fan was the lost work of some famous artist, repaired the omission and added the signature themselves – very clearly.

France

Somewhere in the mid-seventeenth century the French started painting their fans rather than cutting them out of vellum or silver paper (découpé). They were dark in background, decorative in character, very large, very rich, very correct and often very regal. Generally a full painted scene would stretch from one side right to the other with no extra decoration, such as seen in fig. 24. Early French painted fans looked almost as if they could be updated miniatures from a Book of Hours, or a tapestry cartoon such as those produced by Bernard Van Orley. There is one in the Schrieber Collection in the British Museum depicting 'The Marriage of the King with Maria Theresa of Spain', whose only indication that it is in fact a fan leaf is a half-moon left in the scene for the sticks – but even this is minute.

The eighteenth century

By the end of the first quarter of the eighteenth century the style for painting fans in France had altered, and now a central composition on a light background was favoured, surrounded by a full border of foliage and flowers doggedly edging the entire leaf. The colours were bright, there was little gilding seen on the painted leaf, and the artist did his utmost to create a three-dimensional scene, often figures in a landscape.

The style of painting at this time was crisp and economical, like the decoration on porcelain. The artist still treated the leaf as a canvas, rather than trying to create effects with the brush to suggest other materials and textures. A beautiful example is fig. 30

26   Italian fan, c.1700; the vellum mount painted with scenes of nymphs, satyrs, landscape and ruins; the reverse shows a seascape. Sticks of inlaid ivory. Victoria and Albert Museum, Crown copyright

which shows *Une Fête Galante* painted in gouache on paper, showing how much thought was given to the general balance of the composition in order to make it orderly and symmetrical, sober and dignified. Sticks were reasonably simple with rounded shoulders and no really related scene with the leaf or mount. The alternative was to have the brisé types with a Vernis Martin application (see pp. 155-61 and glossary).

Very often the subject matter was from recognizable classical, biblical and mythological stories, but it could also be political. Before the time of the daily newspaper and the general emancipation of women, the ramifications of politics were often extended far within society, and even the fan could be an instrument of political or social intrigue. Nowadays politics are mainly for the professionals, but during the seventeenth and eighteenth centuries politics were the business of everyone with any education and any device was employed to indicate a political interest or bias. One fan made in this period was described in a sale catalogue of 1882:

'The Preliminaries of Peace between Austria and France in 1748. The scene represents a tented field; Maria Theresa, Queen of Hungary, stands by an altar joining hands with another female, representing France; on each side are banners displayed, those of France on the right are grounded and inscribed "Vive le Louis 15th", on the left the English banner of St. George is in front, with those of Spain and Austria, the latter inscribed "Vive la Reine d'Hongrie", river deities on either side; at the back a naval battle, and refers to Admiral Hawke's victory; stick, ivory, sculptured with the same subject, and probably executed for an English patron on the occasion of the Peace.'

As we have seen, in early fans the composition was spread right across the leaf. Interest

27 An early French fan, c.1700. The skin mount shows scenes from Poussin's The Children of Israel dancing round the Golden Calf, *now in the National Gallery, London. Victoria and Albert Museum, Crown copyright*

would be balanced in every section and often the central figures were painted set back in the middleground. Gradually interest in a specific feature began to dominate until the entire theme became central and, to give added weight to the fact, was enclosed in a border; however, the seventeenth-century preoccupation with a heavy floral border, painted, embroidered or carved, around any central theme, related or not, was over. A truly magnificent example of this changing style is the series of mythological figures painted on a chicken-skin leaf in fig. 28. The artist has placed as much importance on the fan's glorious pierced sticks of mother-of-pearl as on its theme of Neptune at the Banquet of the Gods.

By the middle of the eighteenth century not only was the central theme enclosed in a painted border but subsidiary themes were placed in two other circles, ovals or squares on either side. The empty spaces in between were very lightly painted in, cross-hatched or with minute arabesques, lacking the former heavy painting edging all around the leaf as a frame. Sometimes, although this was rare, there would be several vignettes of equal size, as in the mid-century fan of fig. 29.

By the middle of the eighteenth century in France (there are no hard and fast demarcation lines) fan decoration was lifted up onto a lighter, more feminine plane; inspired by Watteau a great many scenes now showed *fêtes champêtres, conversations galantes, moments musicales* and *pastorelles*; that beautiful evocative never-never land of no real people, no real time, no real place. Later on fan painters were as much inspired by Lancret, Pater, Boucher and Fragonard, but it was Watteau who turned the corner for them. This style was often simple and charming, as in fig. 31 with its scene of gentle dalliance with no unnecessary extra details or embellishment.

The leaf painters would take a theme from one artist, a pair of lovers from another, a

rose-decorated piece of classical statuary from a third and marry them with the lightest of touches. They very rarely lifted wholesale from a well-known work of art, and fan leaves by this time were always referred to as being 'in the style of' but never quite. Thus in fig. 32 the composition shows a mixture of Watteauesque types with Gravelot legs and Boucher colouring.

As with the textiles and furniture of the eighteenth century the dark, rich, masculine colours gave way to silvery, feminine ones; compositions were no longer serious and uplifting themes but delightful trivialities and the thin, fine, rococo gold lines came romping in, enlivening the pretty concoctions with delicate asymmetrical scrolling. It is quite easy to tell the difference between mid-eighteenth and mid-nineteenth century gilding – the former is softer, thinner, flatter, and the latter brassier with thick scrolling and a massed effect.

Some Rococo fans are terribly weak and of no consequence, with silly, tricky scenes, colours that are too pale and badly carved sticks, yet some of them are quite magnificent. In art history one tends to laugh at the Rococo period, passing over it quickly because it is not serious enough for the dedicated and literary art historians to contemplate for more than five minutes. This is a pity, since it gives the average person a guilt-complex at enjoying it at all. Much in the decorative arts is exaggerated, capricious and nonsensical, but equally a great deal is enchanting and it was time, anyway, to get away from the ponderous heaviness of the late Baroque.

By now many a fan was being made of painted silk as well as vellum, chicken-skin, or paper, occasionally the vignettes having a border of tiny sequins to give yet another texture to the composition. The fans of the true French Rococo period were made between about 1736 and 1765, although the light asymmetrical scrolling characteristic of the period continued for years in other ways and was brought in again, more heavily,

30 'Une Fête Galante' painted in gouache on paper. Ivory sticks inlaid with tortoiseshell, coloured ivory, engraved mother-of-pearl and silver piqué-work. 1720-30. By courtesy of the Countess of Rosse, Messell Collection

31 *French fan, second half of the 18th century. Mount of painted paper, sticks and guards of ivory, pierced and carved. 50cm. (19½in.). Victoria and Albert Museum, Crown copyright*

during the nineteenth century. Fans were, on the whole, larger than before and there was great demand in France, in the fans without vignettes, to have rather elaborately painted decorations in the corners or spandrels with a coloured background. In both England and Italy fans of this period more often than not had a natural-shade or white background.

When there are medallions, cartouches or vignettes (call them what you will) they are generally of different sizes, the central one being the largest, the subjects in the smaller ones showing related themes (fig. 33), and sometimes, as we have seen, there were four minor vignettes rather than two. An unusually fine French fan of the Neo-classical period has a silk leaf with a central vignette portraying a 'romantic view' and cupids. The colouring of the painted leaves in the late eighteenth-century fans was fresh and gay, the surrounding leaf always in a far lighter tone and the whole effect made to blend with the dress, furnishing fabrics, wall-damasks and porcelain of the period.

32　French fan, 1760. Mount of
painted paper, sticks and guards
of mother-of-pearl, carved and
inlaid. 58 cm. (21 in.). Victoria
and Albert Museum, Crown
copyright

In fig. 40 one can see the special care taken
with the composition to keep the faces of the
major figures without a crease across them,
and with the pale surround and the tortoiseshell sticks. In the Rococo period sticks and
guards which in the past had been simple
had become crisp, sharp, and squared-off.
The carving now was intricate, some of it
quite exquisite with a centralized theme
carved or painted and relating to the leaf
above, presenting an uninterrupted surface
for an expansive scheme of decoration. During
the third quarter of the eighteenth century
the size of the fan began to diminish and, to
make the sticks look less heavy, they were
made far thinner and were spaced apart,
letting in the light just the way that the
furniture styles were opening up the backs
of chairs to make them lighter in every way,
and looking very much like the spokes of
a wheel.

As the sticks were now fewer and less
obviously structural, there was almost more
opportunity to make a feature of them, so

they were carved less as flat segments, all alike, and more in the round and often all different. They could appear one way when open, and a totally different way when shut. It is always imperative to hold a closed fan in the hand for some time before you open it, so as to get its 'feel' and balance and especially to look at the treatment of the sticks when bunched together.

Sometimes the sticks could be so carved as to look like a Chinese scene when shut, like flowers when opened; or the flowers or ribbons carved on individual sticks form a complete garland spiralling all around the guards and sticks when shut, appearing to lock them in place. Another type was the 'Pagoda' stick, composed of long, thin ivory rods, linked at intervals, which were supposed to look like bamboo (very much like Chippendale's carved 'bamboo' legs for his furniture) and which 'scrunch' in the palm (fig. 31). When closed it is still possible to look through the bunched sticks as though there were windows in the middle. At this time in France they were also making and exporting many fans especially for the Spanish market, and concentrated on fancy sticks such as those with alternately curved or pointed sections running down their lengths, or looking, when closed, like perforated spades, hearts, clubs and diamonds from a pack of cards.

On the whole the sticks and guards of the eighteenth century were far the most sophisticated and fancy of all times. They were made from ivory, mother-of-pearl, tortoiseshell, bone, woods and other rigid materials and then encrusted with both silver or gold, or with piqué-work in both precious metals or painted or perforated or carved.

The studs and rivets of eighteenth-century fans bear close examination for in these earlier years the pin was actually rivetted, sent right through, turned back on itself and made impossible to remove after it had been hammered flat; the washers, studs or buttons (all names are valid) were normally of mother-of-pearl or ivory.

33 A French fan, c.1785. The mount is of silk, painted, and with sequins of brass and trimmings of gilt thread. This is a very high quality fan. Victoria and Albert Museum, Crown copyright

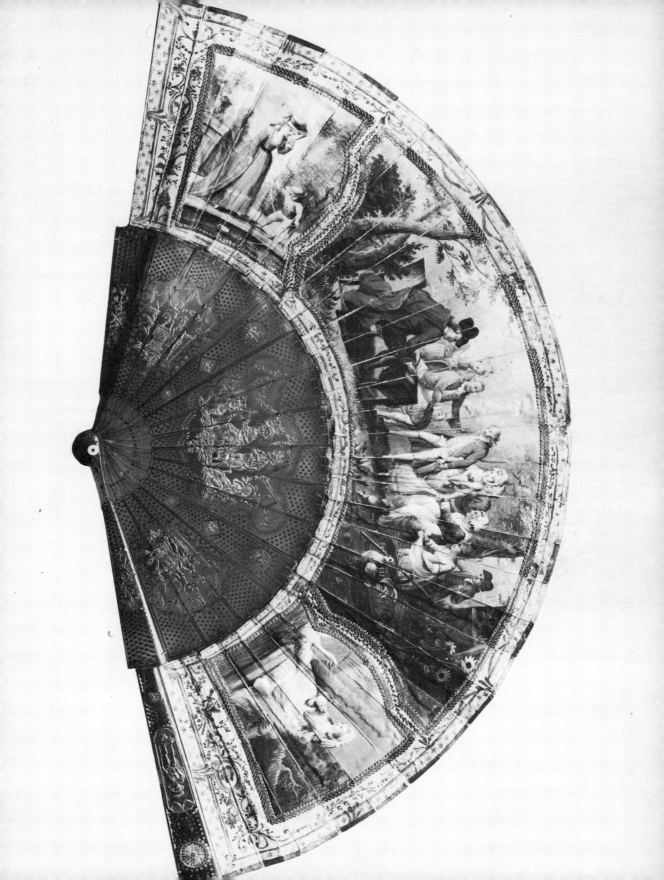

In the eighteenth-century fashion decreed a form of sparkling jewel for the stud, a precious stone, maybe, or paste to match the dress colour of the night; these were placed in cut-down settings (in the next century they were built up like a gallery) and the rivet made in two parts. One part was hollow with the thread turned on the inside, the other part screwed into the first, making it easy to remove or to replace. Should an older fan have had the original type of unmoveable rivet and need repairing, then on occasion the original rivet was forcibly removed and a later, screw-type, rivet replaced it.

Few people take much notice of rivets and metal loops in European fans, partly because they were so easily interchanged but mainly because they are far more interested in the leaf or sticks. If an eighteenth-century fan is found in its original state then it would never have an added metal loop. This style was not introduced until the nineteenth century when many a lady would clutter herself up with a parasol, a reticule, a fan and several other paraphernalia, then, lacking a spare hand, she would slip her fan-loop over a finger or a length of ribbon through the loop would settle on her wrist, so then she could cat's-cradle with everything else.

For one reason or another occasionally loops or slip-on rings were added to earlier fans, together with the multi-coloured ribbons

which would expect to flutter from them, and it is reasonably easy to see if this has been done; Victorian fans should, on the other hand, expect to have the loop attached right from the beginning.

As French art dominated Europe during the Rococo period understandably other countries emulated her, painted their fans in the French styles, copied the more curious and original and added native touches of their own. For instance it was the French who began the idea of adding straw to their decorations, yet it was the Germans who took up this craft and developed it enthusiastically during the eighteenth and nineteenth centuries.

But it was in France that the output and variety of fans were at their greatest; there were plain ones, fancy ones and inventive ones. They followed in the wake of French court fashions, were taken up for a time, elaborated in every possible way and then dropped as a new style came onto the horizon. The themes in paint from the Rococo period onwards switched to contemporary events; royal marriages were honoured, State visits celebrated, family christenings made more memorable, family weddings were never forgotten and fans were made for all Happenings of especial note.

Amongst the loveliest are the romantic marriage fans; when discovered they are in extremely good condition (one only expected to use it the once) as they have been treasured over the years and, indeed, over the generations. They were given as a gift from groom to bride, smaller and less elaborate ones on the same theme were given by the bride to her attendants and chief guests.

Endless time and patience have been lavished on these marriage fans, which became family heirlooms. All female members of the Royal families of Europe had special marriage fans, right up into recent times, the Princess Mary of Teck, afterwards the Queen-Consort of King George VI, received forty for her wedding in 1893.

34 An unusual French fan, c.1780. The silk leaf has a central vignette with a painted 'Romantic View' on applied mother-of-pearl; the reserves are decorated with spangles, sequins and gold braid; the ivory sticks pierced and silvered. 26.5cm. (10¼ in.). By courtesy of Christies

A master fan-maker would create the bride's fan on finest vellum or chicken-skin or silk; the guards and sticks of ivory and mother-of-pearl were very heavily enriched, sometimes jewelled on the guards with a monogram in diamonds—never pearls, they were for 'tears' and boded ill.

The subjects that were used for the painted theme were on the lines of 'The Judgement of Paris', 'Endymion and Diana', 'Antony and Cleopatra', 'The Sale of Cupids', 'The Power of Love', 'The Marriage of Cupid and Psyche' and 'The Sacrifice to Hymen'. If one of these themes were in the central medallion, then the side and smaller medallions would have cheerful little pink cherubs playing hide and seek in paler pink clouds. Then again, amongst the beautifully carved sticks, there would generally be another relating central oval scene, painted or carved or even both, or an impeccably carved monogram of the bride's and groom's initials intertwined.

Amongst the inventive fans, and one of the earliest, was the cabriolet fan, a type, incidentally, which is getting more and more difficult for collectors to track down. The history of this fan exemplifies the integration of the fan into the ever-changing fashion world.

In 1755 a man called Joseph Child, brother of Lord Tilney, introduced to Paris an elegant horse-drawn two-wheeled cart which became the height of fashion and everyone, but everyone, wanted to own a cabriolet. Such was their popularity that cabriolets appeared as motifs in dress as well; Walpole wrote to his friend Mann that 'men had small cabriolets painted upon their waistcoats, embroidered on their coloured silk stockings, and women were muffled up in great caps with cabriolet wheels on them'. Naturally, fans were made to look like these fashionable little carriages as well. The normal single leaf was divided into two to make a cabriolet fan, sometimes with even three rows of material decorated with painted scenes, often showing the proud owner driving her own cabriolet and horses; the smaller number of

35 Cabriolet Fan; the leaf is of painted paper, decorated with figures in a landscape. French 18th century. The Metropolitan Museum of Art, New York, bequest of Mary Strong Shattuck, 1935

sticks which were fashionable at this time are clearly visible running right through, carefully and evenly spaced apart like the spokes of the painted wheels of the carriage (fig. 35).

Eighteenth-century France gloried in refined and jewelled conceits such as a tiny gem-set harp concealing a musical-box, an agate étui with its lid smothered in diamonds and rubies and bound together with gold scrolling, and the scores of glorious jewelled snuff-boxes.

Marie Antoinette was a great giver of these kinds of presents, with her youth and her joie de vivre she brought variety and gaiety to the otherwise monotonous and dull court of Louis XVI. She and her young friends organized festivities, balls, concerts, hunting-parties and picnics, and they were always inventing something fresh to do or to give as presents.

She had a heyday when the future Paul I of Russia visited the French court with his wife in the spring of 1782, for the most brilliant receptions and entertainments were arranged to dazzle them at Versailles, Fontaine-bleu and the Trianon. Marie Antoinette thought up new surprises for the young Arch-duchess every day, together with extravagant presents such as a dressing-table set of Sèvres porcelain in lapis lazuli and gold, every piece marked with the visitor's arms and initials.

The young royal pair were seated together one evening in the charming little theatre at Versailles and a colloquial report continues: 'It seems to me,' the queen suddenly said to the arch-duchess, 'that you are just as short-sighted as I am. But I assist my eyes with a small lorgnette discreetly arranged in my fan. Try it and see if you can see better with it.' Thereupon she handed her her fan, richly decorated with diamonds and other precious stones, and in which a lorgnette was hidden.

By a graceful movement of the fan it could be used as a pair of opera-glasses, without attracting attention to the defective sight of a beautiful woman. The archduchess was enchanted with this invention of a lorgnette fan and was naturally pressed to keep the costly treasure.

Painted fans, political fans, marriage fans, lorgnette fans and a little fan that folded into the shape of a bouquet – they were all the rage for a time and written up with enthusiasm in the journals of the period.

There were plenty for gaiety and happy invention, but what for the sad days? It was quite unthinkable to emerge from your room into society without a fan in your hand, but how on earth could you arrive with love rioting in arbours of roses when at the same time you were choking back floods of tears? Weeping in public was simply not polite to your friends, for they had troubles enough

of their own without you adding to them. It was equally wrong to arrive in deepest black all the time as an unspoken reminder of your sorrows.

No, the answer was to carry a mourning fan which would go well with your mourning clothes of white, grey or lavender. This fan would depict a suitably quiet scene, and there were several standard ones such as 'The Queen of Sheba goes to visit King Solomon'. This would be painted in grisaille (grey monochrome) on a white background, or white on a grey or lavender background (fig. 53).

The fashion for mourning fans lasted as long as the fashion for fans, and most of them have had a good deal of use. Collectors do not become very excited about mourning fans because the quality of the painting is not very high, the colours have to be drab and the whole concept is in direct contrast to the flamboyance usually associated with fans.

Two fans were developed as special aids to flirtatious young ladies at court. These were fans for peeping through, the domino fan and the mask fan, and they are not the same.

The domino fan was perfectly ordinary, often painted to look like velvet or patterned lace. Two small sections were cut out for the eyes so that the fan might be used as a mask, the wearer looking through the holes which were carefully concealed as part of the pattern.

The mask fan was again a perfectly simple folding fan but painted across the whole of the front was a face, as unlike the owner's as possible, the two eyes cut out for the owner's own. Then she would hold it up to her own face and it would be extremely difficult to tell who she was, far more difficult than when a lady wore a fitting domino across the upper part of her face, for a chin can be disastrous give-away. An example is given in fig. 36.

French court life was riddled with elaborate artefacts and elaborate conventions. One of these was that no fan, except her own, could be opened in the presence of the Queen. Should she happen to need some small thing passed to her, a dropped glove, a bonbon, a hair-ribbon to choose, it was handed to her by one of her ladies on her half-opened fan. But for anyone else to use her fan to cool herself down in the stifling rooms – never.

Yet the ennui, the boredom and the cynicism sometimes appeared through their conversations and literature. An anonymous poet of the age produced this philosophical madrigal:

If it be true that from all things we ought,
Finding some good, to live,
You have a very proper subject for your
    thought
Here in this Fan I give.

Its uses will put this query to your mind,
What is the world but wind?

36   Mask fan, the leaf of painted paper. 18th century, Spanish. The Metropolitan Museum of Art, New York, gift of Mrs William Randolph Hearst, 1963

What all the joys which seem to make us
    rich?
What all *we* think so gay?

What are they? what but painted shadows
    which
Pass in a breath away!
The Fan is like our life; it opens wide,
And then is shut, and then is laid aside,

To rest unseen, forgotten and alone,
In it, O fair and sweet sage Sylvia, see
What at the end of life we all shall be:
Nought else, my dear, nought else but
    skin and bone!

This form of 'vapeur' contrasted ill with the other refinements of luxury and high living of the French court during the third quarter of the eighteenth century, but it was there all the same. Cruel little poems, philosophical anagrams, *bons-mots* and theatrical kernels for farces appeared in perfumed notes, whispered behind bejewelled fans and were laughingly declaimed at those 'orgies' of little suppers, breakfasts on the grass, the *déshabillé* of the morning *lévée* and in the general badinage of silly conversations.

Perhaps they could sense how short their lives were going to be, so many of them. Yet it is reported that when the highest-born went, unpowdered, shorn and jeered at in the tumbrils to the guillotine, they stood proud and upright, and none could ever forgive Madame du Barry for not knowing how to die 'as graciously as she had held her fan', crying out 'Only one moment, Mister Executioner; I beg of you, only one moment!'

The nineteenth and twentieth centuries

In the confusion of the early nineteenth century both politics and dress were interwoven, quickly changed and rather austere. Countries neighbouring on France were almost as affected as her by her turbulent affairs.

The phrase, 'What Paris means to the

37   *French fan, mid 19th century. Ivory, carved and gilt, by E. Moreau, painted with three medallions showing scenes of a tournament. Victoria and Albert Museum, Crown copyright*

38   *French fan, c.1885. Pleated skin mount, mother-of-pearl sticks. This shows the Princess Marie d'Orleans on horseback. Victoria and Albert Museum, Crown copyright*

fashionable woman London means to the well-dressed man', was very true at this time; French men came to England for their beautifully tailored clothes and the ladies of England adopted French fashions. During the Empire period (1804-15) very gradually warmer fabrics came into fashion in both countries, starting in France; taffettas, velvets and brocades quietly returned into vogue; the neckline travelled upwards, the sleeve travelled down; white was still predominant as a Republican colour but other shades were coming in together with diamonds, lace, and feathers from rare birds.

Paintings of the period, such as those by Ingres, together with the fashion magazine illustrations show this transition period with ladies posing most self-consciously in neo-Greek positions. Fans were not much painted during the post-Revolution period but were small and as delicate and transparent as some of the fabrics. In France many were 'busy with Imperial bees or strewn with Bourbon lilies' while in England they showed cobwebby white or black net strewn with spangles. However, from the 1820s onwards there was a return to Romanticism in dress as well as architecture, painting and the decorative arts. People were looking backwards and copying the past, gripped in the throes of the machine age which catered for many monied customers with little real discrimination and with muddled aesthetics.

Just before the French Revolution there had been an enormous output of fans, variety being of paramount importance, speed being equally essential and an inevitable drop in the quality of painting is noticeable.

39   Fan designed by Paul Porret
to advertise his Atelier Martine,
1920. By courtesy of Martin
Battersby from his collection.

After a fairly long interval and period of
neglect, the year 1829 saw a revival in the taste
for painted fans. A grand ball was to be held
at the Tuileries in Paris and an especial
feature of the evening was that several
'costume quadrilles' were to be danced.
Madame la Duchesse de Berri had undertaken
to get up a 'Louis xv' quadrille and, to make it
thoroughly effective, she had been searching
for Louis xv fans to be carried by the ladies:
she could find none. Suddenly someone
remembered having seen some old fans in
the shop window of a perfumer named Vanier
who lived in the rue Caumartin.

They went along to see the old man. He had
been collecting old fans for some time as he
thought them so beautiful, but he was prepared to sell them, and they were taken to the
palace for the ball. They were a wild success,
they created a furore, and every one was
purchased in a twinkling.

The Duchesse de Berri's success at the ball
started a renaissance for the painted fan and
from that date until the end of the century,
in certain exclusive circles, the finely made fan
never lost favour. However, no new forms
were attempted, with the passion for the past
the only fans which would sell were those
which imitated older styles, such as a fine
painted ivory brisé fan in fig. 37.

For the collector much trouble has resulted
from nineteenth-century eclecticism, copying
of the past and nostalgia for past glories.
It resulted in a great deal of faking: occasionally scenes were deliberately painted in the
manner of the early and mid-eighteenth
century, then stupidly placed on sticks which
could only have been made during the
nineteenth century; or, alternatively, fan-
makers ripped off an old eighteenth-century
leaf, used the original sticks and then replaced the leaf with a newly painted scene.

The third quarter of the last century saw a
multitude of national and international exhibitions, mounted to promote the advanced
techniques of their machine age. Most of
the ancient crafts had been completely

industrialized and some very interesting facts relating to the manufacture of painted fans appeared in a report of the Délégations Ouvrières of the Paris Universal Exhibition of 1867. This stated that the sticks of fans were especially made in the Département de l'Oise and that mother-of-pearl, ivory, bone, sandalwood and other domestic and foreign woods were used; that the manufacture of mother-of-pearl was carried on in Andeville and the other materials in St Genéviève. It also stated that the work was chiefly domestic, the artisan, his wife and children all taking a hand in it and frequently attaining great skill. The finely painted mount, however, was exclusively of Parisian manufacture. The fans thus produced were made under the direction of the principal dealers in Paris and were of the highest quality, usually representing some speciality which belonged to their producer. 'In England,' the report continued, 'the trade had not found such development, and its future extension would seem to depend upon the uprising there of men of taste and capital, who, as producers and sellers, shall occupy the place of the Paris Éventailliste!'

Most fans were now made of textiles, lace or feathers, but occasionally some fine painted fans were made by commission, such as the fan in fig. 38. This was made in 1885 of a pleated skin mount and shows the Princess Marie d'Orléans on horseback, probably near Chantilly. It is known that two such fans were made at the same time, the one illustrated is in the collection at the Victoria and Albert Museum and the other is in private hands in Denmark.

There were a few fans painted during both the Art Nouveau period and the Art Deco period between the wars. The former are distinguished by a linear patterning with sinuous, sensuous, never-ending lines and beautiful, indeterminate colours of greeny-blues, silvery-golds and pinks shading into oranges. The subject-matter was almost always a copy of a Japanese motif, taken from the artefacts which had poured into the country after Japan had opened her borders to foreigners. Painted Art Nouveau fans, on the other hand, are few and far between. There was little point in painting them as countless cheap fans were flooding the market. The only French ones to attain any success were large and made from very fine black textiles or paper with pseudo-Japanese designs upon them. Their sticks were narrow at one side and widened to twice their length at the other—a typical balancing trick which fitted in well with the distortions of the age.

Fans were used before the First World War but these were made of lace and feathers. Their use declined until after the war life became increasingly commercial. Fans now were used to amuse and to advertise—a hotel, a shop, or a drink—or for atmospheric effect (fig. 50). The fan illustrated in fig. 39 was made to advertise the Atelier Martine, and is autographed by its founder, Paul Poiret. On the reverse is a list of the scents produced by the Parfumerie Rosine. It is a charming gesture which made no pretensions towards fashion styles, expense or artistic achievements with its thin paper and brightly painted plain wooden sticks.

This was the death of the painted fan. Women had work to do, they no longer trailed elegantly about in sweeping dresses but dashed from one jazzy party to the next in their little runabouts, a handbag in one hand, a cocktail and a cigarette in the other. There was no longer room for a fan in their lives.

England

The history of painted fans from England follows roughly the same lines as in Italy and France, matching their size changes, leaf decoration, expansion and contraction, treatment of sticks and adoption of the various novelty forms.

As we have already seen they were much used by Queen Elizabeth I who encouraged her merchant traders to bring luxuries from all over the world for the people of England. Many of the sumptuary laws of the past were abandoned as the wealthy merchant classes indulged in previously unknown extravagances and delights.

By the beginning of the seventeenth century, fashions, dress and manners had become exaggerated and luxurious. Divines thundered against them from the pulpits, to no avail, and it took dire poverty to curb the ladies' ways.

Women at court wore great farthingales and had to counterbalance the width these gave their skirts with scarves, fans and feathers or aigrettes in the hair. (These aigrettes stemmed from the feather headdresses of the past and the fly-whisks, the

40   An early English fan, c.1680. The vellum leaf is dark brown, delicately painted and with tortoiseshell sticks. By courtesy of Christies

curls of ostrich feathers, the standing feather fans, and the jewelled jicquas of Persia and India.)

The fashion for the farthingale was restricted to Western Europe and absolutely fascinated ladies from other lands who had either heard of them or seen them on some occasion. Apparently the Sultana of the Grand Seigneur at Constantinople had heard of these curious European sights, and one day she asked James I's ambassador, Sir Peter Wyche, to introduce his wife to her. She went in great state, buried in her farthingale, to pay her respects. A contemporary report continues:

'The Sultaness entertained her respectfully; but withall wondering at her great and spacious hips, she asked her, whether all English women were so made and shaped about those parts; to which my Lady Wyche replied, that they were made as other women were, withall showing the fallacy of her apparel in the device

41   An early English fan leaf in very good condition, c.1680, showing people of fashion embarking on a ferry-boat. 50 cm. (20 in.) wide. By courtesy of Christies

42   A most interesting topographical English 18th century fan. The leaf is painted with figures before Cliveden House by Joseph Goupy; the sticks are of ivory. By courtesy of Christies

of the verdingale; until which
demonstration was made, the Sultaness
verily believed it had been her natural
and real shape.'

No wonder!

The skirt gradually became less extravagant, fitting round the figure more naturally towards the end of the seventeenth century, but the fans remained quite wide. The one in fig. 41 is all of 55cm. (20in.) across. The quality of its painting is very high. Like the Italian and French fans of the same period the composition has been taken right across the leaf from one side to the other and it shows no framing of flowers or gilded scrolls, both of which were to come far later. The quality of the painting was apparently so good that the fan has never been pleated and mounted upon sticks but treated instead as a landscape with figures and framed like an easel-painting.

Fig. 40 shows a fan contemporary with that of fig. 41, but quite different. The leaf is of vellum and painted an even darker brown than its normal shade and mounted on tortoiseshell sticks, making it a very early example of the use of this material. The painting on the leaf, however, is very delicately carried out in lighter tones – merely a whisper of a composition – and great care has obviously been taken to keep each face clear of pleats. Again there is no border and the leaf is treated like a canvas, but a rectangular canvas, not a shaped one.

Many a political fan was painted at the end of the Stuart succession and the advent of the Hanoverian monarchs in England. The very worthy and adventurous National Association of Decorative and Fine Arts Societies (NADFAS for short) gave a most interesting fan of this type (fig. 77) to the Victoria and Albert Museum recently. It symbolizes the Jacobites' sorrow at the end ·of the Stuart monarchy when Queen Anne died in 1714; the fan quite easily might have been made either then or in 1715 at the time of the First Rebellion. What can be seen,

43   *A curious 18th century painted English fan; the leaf shows an architect accompanying his patron around a new extension to a building. The sticks and guards are of unadorned ivory. By courtesy of Christies*

from left to right, is first the head of Charles II in an oak-tree, then Queen Anne being raised to Heaven holding in her hand a single ostrich feather, the symbol of monarchy. This is followed by the State in mourning, the Stuart Arms and finally the White Rose of the Stuarts with two buds, the whole with a light framing around the upper edge.

The eighteenth century

Late seventeenth and early eighteenth century fans all showed one scene right across the leaf or mount with singing colours and then scrolling baroque forms. One, given by Charles II to the Duchess of Portsmouth, was described in an 1884 catalogue as 'having a skin mount, finely painted and finished, representing Ulysses' before Deidamia with figures, slaves and camels, foliage and buildings. Sticks and guards of mother-of-pearl, inset with gold ornaments; the whole buttoned with a paste rivet. On the reverse a landscape minutely detailed, attributed to Hollar.'

There was no painted border on the leaf to frame the painted scenes, and fans looked as if long, thin paintings had been made, pasted over the sticks and then the leaf cut round the edges to fit them; leaving out a subject's legs or half a tent simply did not matter as long as the final effect was balanced.

Gradually fan-painters realized that they should treat their work quite differently, not as if it were a miniature version of an easel

70 *Painted fans*

painting; and, as paintings which were inset into the architecture within a house came away and were framed, to be hung wherever his will took the owner, so the fan-painters began to frame up their fan leaves. In fig. 43 one can see the tentative beginnings of treating fan leaves in this new style. This depicts an architect accompanying his patron around a new extension to an existing building, but leaves us with the enigma – where is it? The wave of rebuilding during the early part of the eighteenth century was a product of the Grand Tour and the bedded-in wealth of the Whig landowners, so perhaps the acquisition of a fan showing one's own alterations was a little one-up-manship between the owner's wives.

The framing is uneven as though it was a map of the property and the cross-hatching looks like some motifs for plaster ceiling squares. As with all the previous fans of the period the sticks are plain and unadorned.

In the slightly later topographical fan in fig. 42, the framing has begun to develop with flowers shading off to the sides and an extremely light scrolling around the edge. Its ivory sticks are beautifully carved and the fashions depicted in its subject are again interesting. The skirts have widened out once more and are placed on hoops.

Topographical fans such as these are fascinating from an historic as well as an artistic point of view, but it is very rare to find one.

England followed the French styles and fashions slavishly throughout the eighteenth century and their production ran side by side over the novelty fans (mostly begun in France) and the marriage and mourning fans. They also entertained themselves during the nonsensical Rococo period with painting *trompe l'œil* fans to amuse and divert (figs. 44 and 45). Some very fine late eighteenth century fans can be seen in many splendid English stately homes, national and regional museums as well as more modest establishments. A great many of them are historical or

44   An English trompe l'oeil *fan, painted in gouache on paper, dated 1757, signed by John Faber. By courtesy of the Countess of Rosse, Messell Collection*

45   An amusing trompe l'oeil *fan, probably English, c.1760. The mount is painted to simulate lapis lazuli flecked with gold on which appear a variety of objects, the reverse shows a parrot, By courtesy of Christies*

show scenes of monarchy or political triumphs. Fig. 46 is a unique fan, derived from a painting by Zoffany of George III, Queen Charlotte and some of their children. It was engraved and then hand-painted, the sticks are of mother-of-pearl, carved and heavily gilded; the framing is light and delicate and the painting economical but fresh and gay.

At the end of the eighteenth century England was just as much affected as any other European country by the Neo-classical phase, perhaps more so. In all her fine and decorative arts a serious effort was made to emulate the classics very faithfully. Many fine designs for fans were painted by Angelica Kauffmann, an artist much associated with Robert Adam (fig. 48).

At the turn of the century painted fans ceded in fashion to the engraved or etched fans followed by tiny textile fans, and the painted fans were not as popular again until the middle of the next century when they became important again as part of the dress of the time.

46   An English historical fan, quite unique, showing King George III, Queen Charlotte and some of their children, after a painting by Zoffany. Engraved and hand-coloured: sticks of mother-of-pearl, carved and heavily gilded. By courtesy of Miss Esther Oldham

47   Top English or French folding fan, c.1820. The leaf is of fine white silk with an embroidered arcade pattern in gilt spangles, gilt sequins and stamped metals. The sticks and guards of horn with piqué. Bottom English or French folding fan, c.1800. The mount is of cream gauze with embroidered design of cut steels mounted on figures and incised gilt sheet. The sticks of blond tortoiseshell. Victoria and Albert Museum, Crown copyright

The nineteenth century

Fashions changed quickly in the nineteenth century, not always for the better, and they went from one extreme to the other. Too many people had too much freedom of choice; clear direction did not really come any longer from the connoisseurs in Society and the resulting confusion was often pin-pointed by the fashion magazines who, with enthusiasm, wrote up every new style and accessory in turn and so added to the lack of fashion confidence. In the memoirs of Maria von Bunsen, quoted in the *Pictorial Encyclopedia of Fashion* (Hamlyn 1968) one receives an idea of the multitude of 'musts' a Victorian lady needed:

'I was full of pleasurable anticipation of my journey to Cannes when I packed my bits and pieces. Packing then was a much more complicated business than it is today. I carefully considered how many parasols would be sufficient for my visit: a practical solid one; a simple one; a brightly coloured one; a good one in coloured silk which would go with my best street costume; an airy one; and a decorated one to match my elegant afternoon gown. That would have to do.

A whole pile of veils, both heavy and light, was prepared; a whole heap of gloves were needed for different occasions. The packing of each dress, with the exception of hard-wearing sports clothes, was a highly complicated matter. Ruches, frilly wraps, flounces, full sleeves, skirts lined with stiffened gauze and underlayed with balayeuses [dust ruffles] needed space; the hat-boxes grew always more voluminous. But all that was necessary.'

Consider the complicated selection of fans she would have needed! The favourite accessories at that time were fans and parasols, and no female hand was ever seen

48 A design for a fan by Angelica Kaufmann, showing the Fine Arts, Painting, Architecture, and Sculpture, with grotesques. Late 18th century. Victoria and Albert Museum

49 The Lafayette Fan, made to celebrate the Marquis de Lafayette's visit to Salem, Mass., in 1824. By courtesy of Miss Esther Oldham

50 Paper fan from the Château de Madrid, from a design by Paul Iribe. This design was parodied by Michael Arlen in **The Green Hat**, *1924: 'the magically white faces of women, the lights in the night making* love to the black shadows in their hair, their lips red as lobsters, their armpits clean as ivory, the men talking with facile gestures, the whole tapestry of the Château de Madrid like a painted fan against a summer night'. By courtesy of Martin Battersby, from his collection

CHÂTEAU DE MADRID

without the one or the other, sometimes both. And now, having shrunk in the eighteenth century, fans had another turn of being enormous. In fact, they went up and down in size in tune with that of the crinoline, and they followed their colours as well. Unhappily much was made that was essentially coarse. The paintings showed scrolling designs of flowers, especially of the convolvulus (Albert's favourite) and the sticks showed heavy scrollings too.

The eclectic phase was upon the English just as much as the other countries, and with this came the faking of fans, or, to be more charitable, the modelling of fans on the older styles. One has to look out for this when collecting and this is where a knowledge of genuine eighteenth-century fashions and hair-styles is essential. Many a Victorian artist did not take enough care with these details or painted the scene in too fussy a manner with brassy gilding and too much decoration. The experts can spot this every time, especially those who have a knowledge of the painting techniques of the period; they can point out the over-enthusiastic artist's work, the looseness of brushwork compared to the crisp and economical style of eighteenth-century artists and the general over-romanticizing of the landscape compositions. It is as well to study the early porcelain of the period, then compare it with the painted fans and finally with a similar fan of the Victorian era. The difference is generally easy to spot after that.

At this time the sticks thickened up and had a mass of gilding and decoration upon them. Many of them were twice as thick in section as their eighteenth-century counterparts, some partly because of the weight of the leaf: these could be so laden with decorations that they would have snapped slender sticks in half. They were also made thick when two leaves were pasted on top of each other, sometimes as a form of restoration. They needed to be sturdy as well because the textiles in high Victorian times

52   English fan-leaf, unmounted, of silk and hand-painted with a scene of Queen Victoria's Ball of 1853. By courtesy of Miss Esther Oldham

were heavy in themselves.

Now it was possible to have a painted (but weighty) linen or cretonne for the leaf, taffetas sparkling with sequins or lustrous silks sewn with braids and embroideries, all lushly advertizing the wealth of the owner in the same manner as their sweeping crinolines and jewellery of diamonds and dark-coloured precious stones.

This was also the age for commemorative objects, souvenirs in jewellery or china or glass or wood, and commemorative fans as well. Two of these – one French, one English and both almost unique – are in the Esther Oldham collection. Fig. 49 shows a 'Lafayette' fan, made in France for Sarah Derby, the wife of the famous ship-owner of Salem, Mass. It commemorates the Marquis of Lafayette's visit to Salem in 1824, and shows the crossed flags of France and America, the sacrificial altar, the Phrygian cap, and the monogram 'S.D.' twice. Its central scene depicts a group of people welcoming a stranger to their shores and is supposed to be an allegorical scene probably signifying the return of

Lafayette to America. Flanking either side in the smaller vignettes are figures representing 'Justice'. The sticks are ivory and terminate in a diamond paste pin.

The other commemorative fan (fig. 52) shows an unmounted fan leaf of silk with a hand-painted scene of Queen Victoria's Costume Ball of 1853. On the left one can see Empress Eugénie seated, and on the right Queen Victoria, and there are apparently more than seventy-five minute colourful figures painted on a cream-coloured background.

These are rare examples. Connoisseurs of fans in England during the latter half of the nineteenth century despaired that no painted fans were being made comparable to the century before. As a result various exhibitions were mounted to try and interest the trade and the craftsmen and women in making fine fans again. In particular, a loan exhibition was mounted at the South Kensington Museum, now the Victoria and Albert Museum, in 1870. But the people's interest was still orientated towards the past rather

53 *English mourning fan,
c.1750. The vellum mount is
painted with a scene in grisaille.
The ivory sticks and guards are
carved and painted in imitation
Chinese style.*

*English folding fan, c.1746.
The pleated mount is printed with
a battle scene, probably the
Battle of Culloden; a General
(understood to be Cumberland)
is seen receiving the surrender of
a young man, presumably a
Jacobite. The sticks are of wood,
the ivory guards are roughly
daubed with Chinoiserie subjects
in colours. This is an early
example of a fan with a printed
leaf. Victoria and Albert Museum,
Crown copyright*

than the present, and enormous enthusiasm was aroused for the magnificent work carried on by other countries and in other times. Basically this exhibition was part of the scheme of the Department of Science and Art for the 'Art Instruction of Women'. To promote this object the Department offered prizes in competitions for fans painted by the students in the Female Schools of Art in 1868 and 1869. The biggest draw was a prize offered by Queen Victoria, who loved romantic fans; she offered £40 for the best fan exhibited, being either a work of painting or carving or a combination of both, and executed by a 'female artist' under the age of twenty-five. Lady Cornelia Guest and Baroness Meyer de Rothschild each offered a prize of £10 for the two next best fans, and, in all, five hundred and three fans were exhibited.

Unhappily, it was no great success: no new and thriving industry came from this, and the dying trade could not be rekindled. However members of the British 'bulldog breed' were loath to give up, and kept trying to start up the industry again, especially when it was reported that three million fans were exported from Japan in 1875 and that one million were ordered for the exhibition at Philadelphia. They were being made in France and Germany and the Spanish could not make enough of them, surely there was some way in which the industry in England could begin again?

One man tried very hard. A report in *The Queen* of 1878 said:

'Mr. E. Barrington Nash, the indefatigable advocate of artistic fan-painting, is going to start a school of this fascinating branch of pictorial art at the Windsor Gallery, 26 Savile Row. The object of this school is to provide profitable employment for the gentlewomen of artistic ability, and to retain some portion of the £100,000, which enormous figure represents the value of the annual import of fans of an artistic character into England. Mr. Nash, by his own work, has given ample proof that he is the right man to manage and superintend the intended school, and the premises he secured are excellently situated for exhibitions, and well adapted for studios. It is most desirable that fan-painting as an industry should be revived in this country; and, therefore, the undertaking of Mr. Nash deserves every possible encouragement.'

But it made no difference, and the project was doomed from the start. Encouraging industry was one thing, having an historic exhibition was quite another. People had flocked to those ever since their interest and enthusiasm had been awakened by the Great Exhibition of 1851.

One of the best exhibitions was put on in 1877 at the Liverpool Art Club in Myrtle Street, which gave a far more comprehensive show of fans in general than had ever been seen before in England. There were sixty-three contributors showing one hundred and seventy-six fans of immense interest: fans from Ancient Egypt, India, Fiji, Burma, Malta, Ceylon, Holland, Italy, France, England and with twenty-four from Japan and thirty-six from China.

The catalogue was lyrical in its descriptions of some of the famous Flemish fans and many from Brazil, those fans of feathers from humming-birds and decorated with flowers made from iridescent beetles' backs. One especial one was 'formed of the feathers of the scarlet flamingo and Brazilian grey hawk, ornamented with the swallow-tailed humming-bird and flowers of beetles' wings'. This type of thing appealed far more to the average English person because they were far more fascinated with craft than with art, especially during the Victorian age, and this is one of the reasons why the major books on fans were written during the last quarter of the nineteenth century. After 1910 there was only one more major book about them, followed by a few articles in magazines, and then fans passed gently into the shadows as romantic antiques.

The last gasp of an exhibition was in 1878 and mounted by the Worshipful Company of Fan Makers at Drapers' Hall in the City of London.

The exhibition was both a wild success and a dismal failure. Unfortunately the organizers were only permitted a total of eight days to exhibit a masterly collection of fans from all over the world. Obviously they had had troubles at the start as it was reported later, 'the arrangements had been so much improved since the opening day by procuring a better light by the aid of gas, and by bringing order into chaos, that one could really enjoy now the magnificent collection, and study its prominent specimens with comfort'.

One thousand, two hundred and eighty-four fans were shown. There were twenty-one prizes awarded together with thirty diplomas. They thought of everything including the lessons learnt from the Great Exhibition of 1851 over entrance fees; for the first two days the entrance fee was two shillings and six-pence, for the rest of the exhibition it was one shilling and from six o'clock to eight in the evening on two days the prices came tumbling down to sixpence, 'so that technical education might be encouraged among the masses'.

Had the exhibition lasted three months it would have paid hand over fist. As it was their receipts for entrance fees and catalogues came to £374.18.0 while their expenses amounted to £1275.0.2. There has never been another comparable exhibition since. From now on the making of painted fans was very rare in England; yet a certain section of the public, the Aesthetes and lovers of the Art Nouveau, became extremely interested in acquiring and copying painted fans from Japan. Many an artist in both France and England, towards the end of Victoria's reign, painted women carrying fans. Most notable was Whistler (1834-1903), who was very much affected by the Japanese art and decorative arts which were flooding into the country. He showed shadowy quiet women with both folding Japanese and fixed Chinese fans, very different from the earliest pictures by Ingres who also painted women with fans, folding and fixed, but in a colourfully high Victorian manner.

This was the end of the serious painted fan from England; in fact it became almost a joke. There are several amusing contemporary drawings in *Punch* showing the inconvenience suffered by men through their ladies and their huge painted fans, being jabbed in the eye, poked in the ear and having their view totally obscured at theatres and social gatherings.

Fans continued in use in England until the 1930s, but descriptions of the gowns at the courts of King George V in 1932, for instance, all show that they were either of feathers or textiles. We have, it seems, gone a full circle.

The Low Countries, Germany, Switzerland

By the seventeenth century the Dutch had established themselves as the main traders in the Far East, bringing back the rarer and more exotic materials for fans. This century is dominated by the successful exploits of the newly emerged Dutch nation – successful because they made no attempt at all to try and convert the Oriental to the Christian faith (which the Portuguese had attempted to do and had proved to be their downfall) but impressed them instead with their diligence and fair dealings.

Their trading all over the world was reflected in their way of life, most graphically seen in the Rijksmuseum in Amsterdam. Here the whole history of the country is panoramically shown in all its complexities: its trading companies abroad and at home; its courts of Elders rather than those of royal personages and pomp; its clean, neat, small houses with

no hint of poverty; its quiet acceptance of the imported luxuries such as brass and carpets from the Middle East, porcelain from China, exotic fruits from Mediterranean countries, parrots from South America, silver from the New World, tulips from Turkey and the leather maps on the walls, which remind us of their new trade routes.

Their great forte in the world of the decorative arts was flowers. They are seen everywhere, in stone, in wood, in textiles and in paint; these flowers were also a reference to the new plants they were bringing back from all over the world which had never been seen by European eyes before. In fig. 54. one can see the emphasis that is put upon them in a very fine mount for a folding fan of painted leather.

The Dutch brought Oriental fans from the Far East to Europe and the materials, too, for making up fans at home, such as perfumed woods, exotic feathers, translucent tortoiseshell and silken, slippery mother-of-pearl.

Everyone in Europe was filled with curiosity over the Far East and what it contained; on one occasion Louis XIV gave the Duchesse de Bourgogne a Chinese fan imported by the Dutch with the accompanying poem:

To chase in summer-time the busy flies,
To keep from cold when suns too quickly
    fade,
China, Princess, here offers you its aid,
In very gallant wise. I fain had offered
    gifts of other sort
To chase all flatt'ring dull fools from the
    Court
Such present had outshined
The rest; but this the crown
Of gifts most worth renown
It seeks but cannot find.

It is interesting to see here how fans were still thought of primarily as fly-whisks.

The Baroque reached a high point in the Netherlands in the seventeenth century and during that century and the following one

some very fine Dutch fans were made and some wonderful ones still remain locked in private collections. Other fine ones can be seen in the Rijksmuseum in Amsterdam, the Boymans van Beuningen Museum in Rotterdam and the Central Museum in Utrecht, either painted, brisé or in lace.

In form Dutch fans were on exactly the same lines as the French and English. They differed in their painted decoration, showing, for instance, the Dutch settlements in places such as Batavia or scenes 'in the Chinese taste' which were a great deal more authentic than those shown by most other European countries, coming nearer to the original because they were so personally involved with the East. During the eighteenth century Dutch and Flemish fans joined in with the normal display of classical taste, mythology or Scriptural history. 'Rinaldo in the Garden of Armida', 'Jacob and Rachel', 'Abraham entertaining the Three Angels' and especially the adventures of 'The Israelites and the Red Sea' are featured on their fan leaves. In fig. 55 one sees an early Flemish fan (c. 1710) with a mount of chicken-skin painted on the one side with a scene of 'Rinaldo in the garden of Armida' and on the other are some beautifully painted flowers. There is a tentative Asiatic touch of a camel peeping out of a tent and the sticks and guards are of etched mother-of-pearl, overlapping with rounded shoulders.

Painted ivory brisé fans from the Netherlands are fairly numerous. Some delightful ones show tiny painted flowers, wriggly insects, downy bees and iridescent butterflies on the blades, very much as if a painting by Walscappelle had come to life. In fig. 56 one can see just such a fan which features birds as well, the flowers being echoed in the carving of the sticks. The ivory is fretted and flat-pierced to look like an edging of lace in many cases, most reasonably so as they had a reputation for marvellously gossamer laces and they were keen to promote this.

Very often the sticks and guards of Netherlandish fans were of a higher quality

54   Dutch fan leaf, c.1700. Made of leather, painted in oil colours and gold and silver, depicting 'Venus, cupids, landscape and flowers'. Victoria and Albert Museum, Crown copyright

55   An extremely early Flemish fan, c.1710. The mount of chicken-skin is painted with a scene of 'Rinaldo in the Garden of Armida'; sticks and guards of etched mother-of-pearl. Victoria and Albert Museum, Crown copyright

than the leaf, for they were wonderful at carving these, just as they were renowned for their brilliance in their carving of wood. Wood-carvers were not only concerned with making splendid guards and linking scenes on the sticks and marrying them to the painted details, but they made a special feature of producing yet a third scene when the fan was closed, making the entire stick look like a Chinese pagoda, for instance, or as an open-work honeycomb.

German fans show no distinct characteristics except for the fact that some seem heavier than their French or English counterparts. They were made with the same forms, the same types of painted decoration. They broke no new ground. However, some were more elaborately gilded in the nineteenth century, some show more in the line of straw-work

than most other nations, and they occasionally use a technique whereby a painted subject is cut out and then laid on net or lace. In fig. 57 there is a very fine German fan of about 1760; the silk leaf is painted with figures and flowers within formal arbours of straw-work, mother-of-pearl and sequins; the ivory sticks are carved, pierced, silvered, gilt and applied with mother-of-pearl and straw-work trophies. It is obvious that an enormous amount of work has gone into this – which is typical of German workmanship – but it appears (although well-balanced) rather heavy for the Rococo period, especially as it is only 26 cm. (10½ in.) wide.

The Germans very rarely scrimped on materials. Their fans have a rich and lushly coloured scene when painted, their craftsman-ship and construction being invariably correct and enduring (they were always made to last and last), but there is always the under-lying feeling that the German nation did not really care for such frivolities and felt them rather unworthy. They preferred to import French or English fans on the whole, but if they were going to make any themselves they had to be the best. A great many were made for home consumption, some being extremely grand and still in private hands.

H. F. Holt, writing in the *Journal of the Archaeological Association* of 1870 about eighteenth- and nineteenth-century fans con-cludes with a description of the Duchess of York's German fan which she used on her arrival in England: 'a pleated fan entirely of diamonds, with an ivory stick pierced and set with diamonds in a mosaic pattern; the outside ones were set with a single row of diamonds, whilst very large brilliants fastened the fan at the bottom'. No doubt it was considered a pretty trifle then, but it shows rather neatly how little the Germans skimped on materials.

The fan in fig. 58 presents another novelty, articulated guards. The carved and gilt ivory sticks are fewer than of earlier fans, and more spaced apart. The guards each have two small scenes painted upon them. To the left of the guard is a tiny little rod which, when activated, moves the arms and legs of the people in the scenes. In France at this same time they were producing fans with a hole in the centre, behind which there was a revolving drum. With a turn of the handle whole scenes could change, but they were cumbersome and did not last for long. Articulated guards were far better.

German fans are never simple and have a mass of details. The Crown Princess Elizabeth of Prussia once gave Queen Victoria a splendid fan which must have appealed to her enormously. It was painted in Coblenz and shows on the face of the mount seven painted compartments, each divided by a gilt trellis covered with flowers: in each compartment there was an architectural view with the names of the buildings underneath—Osborne,

56 Dutch 18th century carved and painted ivory brisé fan. Victoria and Albert Museum, Crown copyright

Overleaf
57 German fan, c.1760. The silk leaf is painted with figures and flowers within formal arbours of straw-work, mother-of-pearl and sequins; the ivory sticks carved, pierced and silvered. By courtesy of Christies

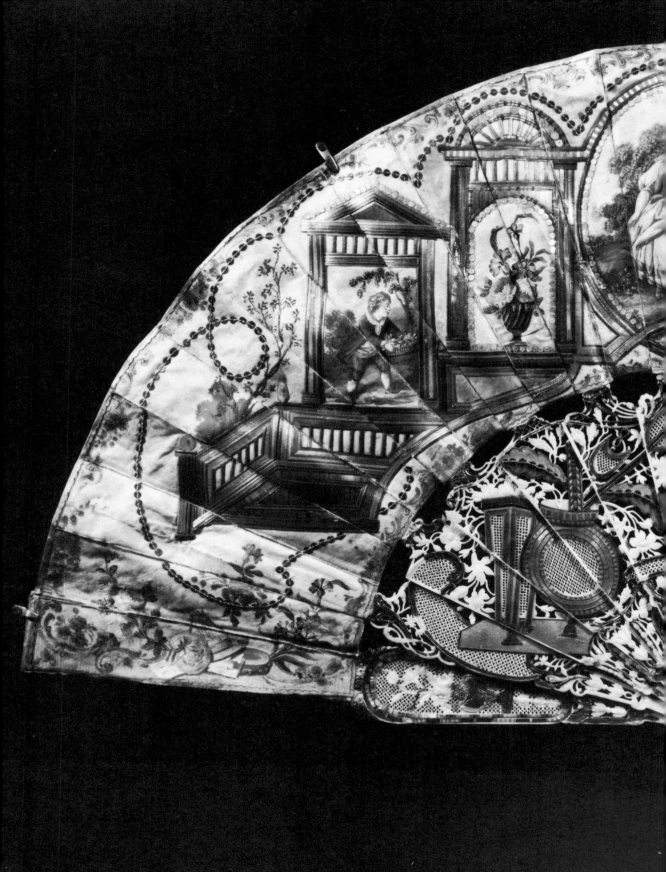

Babelsberg, Buckingham House, Windsor Castle, Coblenz, Balmoral and Berlin. On the reverse of the mount were two monograms 'A.V. 1852 Andenken' (her full Christian names began with Alexandrina Victoria) and 'God Bless You', together with a lozenge showing 'St George and the Dragon'.

The Germans managed to cover their fans with a multitude of decorations and they often made a special feature of the guard-sticks. In one in the possession of Queen Victoria the guards were extended far beyond the length of the leaf and carved into a blackamoor's head which was profusely jewelled. A report mentioned that, in 1823, the Berlin Court jewellers made a bridal fan for the same Crown Princess of Prussia of 300 brilliants and 255 small rose-cut stones. When she eventually died, as Queen of Prussia, she left in her will a fan whose blades

58 *German articulated fan, c.1770. The leaf is painted with a scene of 'The Gods on Olympus', the ivory sticks are carved and gilt. By courtesy of Christies*

Right
59 *Fan painted by Oskar Kokoschka for Alma Mahler, 1913, Museum für Kunst und Gewerbe, Hamburg*

60 *Fan painted by Oskar Kokoschka for Alma Mahler, 1914. Museum für Kunst und Gewerbe, Hamburg*

were set with sapphires and pearls with
matching ornaments, to be left as heirlooms
for the House of Hohenzollern for ever.

It comes as quite a shock to see the simple
fans painted by Oskar Kokoschka for Alma
Mahler in 1913 and 1914 (figs. 59 and 60).
Born in 1886, of Czech and Austrian parentage
and growing up in Vienna, he became known
as a particularly vehement and revolutionary
painter and playwright. Viennese painting
had sunk to a low level during the nineteenth
century, and had then blossomed luxuriantly
during the Art Nouveau years around 1900.
Kokoschka was one of those who rejected the
artificiality of Art Nouveau and placed great
emphasis on the closeness of art to everyday
life, its tensions and conflicts as well as its
beauty, and painted a number of politically
symbolic works. These fans were painted for
Gustav Mahler's wife and are equally symbolic; they can be seen in the Museum für
Kunst und Gewerbe in Hamburg. No fans
are known to have been made after this
period of the First World War in Germany
and, as can be seen, they are very much on
the same lines (of simple folding paper leaf
and even more simple wooden sticks) as the
advertising fans in England and France of the
same time.

One cannot really speak of a fan industry in
Switzerland. All one can do is to pin-point
some fans known to have been made in the
country; the artists who painted the leaves
being either Italian-Swiss, German-Swiss or
French-Swiss and painting in their own
native styles. Two illustrations here are of
considerable interest. A design for a fan
produced in 1775 (fig. 61), one out of a set
of four, is painted in body colour on vellum
and shows figures in fancy dress at a musical
evening; it is inscribed faintly on the reverse.
It shows how little some fan-painters were
still thinking of a fan design as being shaped:
once this had been fitted to the sticks of a fan
about five legs would have to be chopped
off and some windows and walls. The design

*61 Swiss design for a fan,
painted in bodycolour on vellum
with figures in fancy dress at a
musical evening, c.1775.
By courtesy of Christies*

*62 A very delicate 18th century
Swiss fan, c.1780. The leaf is
painted with scenes from country
life and is decorated with two
straw-work bird-cages, so the
fan might be used as a Domino
fan. The sticks are carved ivory,
silvered. It is signed 'peint et
monté par F. Sulzer au Rossignol
à Winterthur'. By courtesy of
Christies*

63. Spanish fan, first half of the 19th century. Painted medallions on glazed paper, mother-of-pearl sticks with gold inlay. Victoria and Albert Museum, Crown copyright

is very highly coloured and full of animation, the wigs of the musicians being the correct shade of pale grey rather than the white most people look for today, which is wrong.

The other Swiss fan (fig. 62) is far more delicate. Made around 1780 the leaf is painted with scenes from country life (the 'back to Nature' phase) and the sticks are carved ivory which are silvered. One of the features of the fan is that it is virtually a domino fan, for the two little hanging baskets (which are made from delicate net) are cut out for the eyes to peep through. If one did not know that they were lashes moving behind the cages they

would be taken for tiny birds.

On the whole Swiss fans are identified purely through their signatures rather than through any special native differences from other European countries.

Spain

The Romantic French writer, Theophile Gautier, wrote in *Tra Los Montes* of the importance of the fan in Spain:

64 *Spanish fan of the first half of the 19th century. Painted in colours on vellum, ivory sticks. Victoria and Albert Museum, Crown copyright*

'The fan corrects in some measure the pretensions of the Spaniards to Parisianism. A women without a fan is a thing I have never yet seen in that favoured land; I have seen women wearing satin shoes without any stockings, but they had, nevertheless, their fans, which follow them everywhere, even to church, where you meet groups of all ages, kneeling or sitting, praying and fanning themselves with equal fervour.'

So indispensable was the fan in Spain that the majority of small collectors have an underlying feeling that Spain was famed for her fans, and that she was a great producer of fans. In fact, Spain imported many of her fans from France, and her own industry was not established until 1802, in Valencia. Before that date only a few fans were made in Spain.

The French made a special point of producing fans which would appeal to the Spanish temperament, the colours very rich and bright, the pleats few and very wide, the sticks spaced apart, the weight heavy so that the graceful Spanish ladies would be forced to wave their fans languidly and with great stylish presence.

One of the characteristics of Spanish fans is that they have always been, on the whole, slightly larger in size, darker in tone and heavier than those from other European countries—mainly made to counterbalance the height of the mantillas and the width of the skirts. One of the most popular types of eighteenth-century 'Spanish' fan, the battoir fan, is heavy with its sticks broadening out in a way which, in the most typical examples, resembles a racket.

On the whole, their bulk prevents Spanish fans from being as beautiful as French or Italian ones. However, there have been some notable exceptions in exhibitions and many more fine handsome fans are known to be secretly closeted in private collections. Those fans never lacked for coats of arms emblazoned on shields and elaborate inscriptions, and they exhibited a far more Italianesque form of painting than anything created by Velasquez or Murillo.

Favourite scenes depicted royal grandeur or political triumphs such as treaties signed or battles won. One fan for instance, which matches up to any masterpiece in another country, shows King Carlos III triumphantly entering Naples in 1743 when he was elected to the Crown of the Two Sicilies. Another shows the capture of the Balearic Islands by Spain in 1759. Not nearly as grand but still very attractive and certainly rather different from many Spanish fans is fig. 63. Its original catalogue entry gives the date 'probably first quarter of the nineteenth century' but this has recently been queried. The fan shows painted medallions on glazed paper and has mother-of-pearl sticks with a gold inlay. The decoration shows Baroque (coming into Rococo) cartouches, the central one with Phillip V of Spain (1683-1746) as their first Bourbon King. Perhaps Phillip here is trying to bring a little bit of France into Madrid by using a Rubens theme, for the decoration is reminiscent of the Marie de Medici series.

65 *Spanish folding fan, early 19th century. The mount is of paper which is painted with water-colours and gilt—the sticks and guards of ivory are carved and pierced and decorated with red metal foil.*

Spanish folding fan, mid 19th century. The mount is of paper with stipple engraving brightly painted in body colour—the sticks and guards are of painted satin-wood—the reverse of the fan shares the same ladies of fashion walking away. Victoria and Albert Museum, Crown copyright

It looks as if he is bringing in all the gods to help him with his work there, notably Minerva who is seen teaching in the left-hand cartouche.

In Spain, as in the traditions of the Orient, there was a fan for every occasion, in the home, the street, the bull-fight, the theatre or the church. Above all, Spanish fans had to be made so they could be open and shut more swiftly than those from any other country because they were manipulated so brilliantly. They were a part of behaviour and conversation; they were spoken with in a whisper or a shout, and they seemed to take on the very personality of their owner. Because of this importance of rapid motion they were reversible and were made to open from either the right or the left.

Any Oriental fans in the country were not officially imported (not until 1889, that is) but must have been individually brought in as a curio from another country. They mostly preferred their own rather insular styles in colours and materials; black or dark red textiles or painted scenes, the sticks and guards often being of a native bog oak. When they used paper it was stout, silk was thickly lustrous. Silk was used lavishly and they enjoyed scented leathers or scented pads between the textile leaves. Spanish fans are the only ones in eighteenth-century Europe which sometimes came to curved points all along the edge of the leaf. This fashion had been seen in sixteenth-century découpé fans (Henri III's, originally at the Cluny Museum, came up to straight points), and during the early nineteenth century all over Europe for a short while there were those, generally small, which looked like little architectural crockets.

The quality of the painted decoration in Spanish fans is generally poor, but they had other outstanding features. The Spanish went in for shapes and forms which other countries did not use. They also had a rather obvious sense of the ridiculous: in the Victoria and Albert Museum there is one dark Spanish

66 Spanish fan, painted mount, painted ivory sticks; first half of the 19th century. Victoria and Albert Museum, Crown copyright

67 Spanish fan, first half of the 19th century with a painted vellum mount and encrusted ivory sticks. Victoria and Albert Museum, Crown copyright

68 *Spanish fan, first half of the*
19th century. Painted paper
mount and mother-of-pearl sticks.
Victoria and Albert Museum,
Crown copyright

fan showing brightly painted ladies in the
latest fashions, reverse the fan to show the
other side and you see the same ladies walking
away with the backs of their dresses on show
(fig. 65); another shows the front and back
views of a dog.

At the end of the eighteenth century and the
beginning of the nineteenth they produced
many fans with the leaf and sticks oddly
proportioned. Normally the leaf is twice the
length of the uncovered portion of the sticks,
or *vice versa*, or, at any rate, proportionately
different in such a way as is comfortable to

the eye – but this is rarely so with the Spanish
fan of the period. One fan has a narrow
leaf, showing a Chinese scene dashingly
painted by a land-locked Spaniard, and sticks
which were two and one fifth times its width,
with painted flowers and insects. Another
has sticks one and one sixth the length of the
leaf; in another the border, heavily painted
with an unrelated theme, is one ninth the
size of the leaf, and yet another with its leaf
three sevenths the length of the sticks.
Somehow the rule of perfect proportions
developed in France and England during

69 Spanish fan, paper mount,
mother-of-pearl sticks; first half
of the 19th century. Victoria and
Albert Museum, Crown
copyright

the Golden Age of the eighteenth century, did not penetrate, with any conviction, south of the Pyrenees. Figs. 63 to 67 all show Spanish fans with curious proportions to their leaves and sticks, and in only fig. 68 are the proportions normal.

The proportion of sticks to unfurled space is occasionally odd as well; one fan which opens up to half a circle has as few as six sticks, making the pleats very wide indeed, showing ten separate scenes which were totally unrelated to each other and having sticks whose width was out of proportion to the spaces in between.

Then again, the shapes of the sticks can be curious. Many are flat-pierced with designs unknown in accepted pattern-books, having little scrollings of fern-like shapes; thin 'C' shapes set at curious angles with the outside edge saw-toothed; little odd-shaped dots and curved marquise-shaped holes like elongated diamonds. In figs. 64 and 69 one can see some of these curious shapes and scrolls in a small way, all unrelated to geometry.

In the poorer types one often receives the impression that well-meaning amateurs were roughly following the lines of the striations of the ivory or wood, working downwards towards the head of the stick and apparently finding it difficult to carve away from themselves and upwards to the leaf.

The Spaniards worked a fair amount in the most difficult of materials, mother-of-pearl, where there is very little 'give'. It is extremely brittle and can easily shatter – but when the light catches it it attracts attention at once (figs. 63, 68 and 69). They also used a technique known in France as *mosaique*, the sticks having a perforated ground and solid reserves carved in bas-relief, quite often backed with another material such as coloured foils, lapis lazuli or gold which is seen through the perforations. They looked very rich, very grand and very colourful and appealed to the conservative taste of the Spanish ladies of society, the quality being so good that at times it is tempting to believe that they were imported from either France or Holland.

On occasion the Spanish used either white bone or dark-toned and polished wood for their sticks. They were flat, with an undulating wavy edge or with edges which came out now and then in a curve to a point, dipping in again and out again to another point. These were either left plain or painted, two white and then one scarlet all round; or with a floral design, very free-hand and loose, lacking any crispness or apparent purpose; two sticks were painted one way, the next another and then the next two a duplicate of the first pair, or each alternate stick was utterly different. It all appealed to their sense of colour and their syncopated rhythms and movements. It is not ungenerous to comment on Spanish fans in the above fashion, for the splendour of the eighteenth-century Spanish fan is a myth. The best of the Spanish eighteenth-century fans were imported from France or Holland because their own were simply not good enough for the top rank of society, and were only used by the average person who wanted to cool herself just as much as the Infanta. Even so, absolutely splendid Spanish fans were made during the nineteenth century, and have continued to be made until the present day; at the last count there were two firms in Seville making them, six in Barcelona and fourteen in Valencia. But then, with their climate, they certainly need them, and it is difficult to see why their industries should ever close down.

Printed fans

England

The fashion for printed fan leaves first arose in England, towards the end of the 1720s. On examination the earlier printed fans appear both simple and rather crude, the scenes badly drawn and the colours randomly daubed on. However, matters improved considerably after 1740, and were even better after 1760. Now the earliest prints are extremely rare for, within a lifespan, printed fans had improved so much that the older ones were destroyed; besides, the subject-matter on each was so ephemeral that the older ones looked old-fashioned (a terrible crime in the Georgian age!).

Some people mistake an etched fan for one decorated with a pen-and-ink design with colour added. The latter would be hand-made and unique, but an etched design can be impressed or printed again and again from the same plate, saving time and money. Firstly a design is made; then a sheet of copper is coated with a specially prepared varnish and the design is scratched onto it with a special needle, the lines going right through the varnish to the copper underneath. The plate is put into a bath of acid which eats into the copper where the varnish has been scratched away. Then it is rinsed clean, the extra varnish removed as well and printers' ink is rubbed into the sunken lines. A piece of paper is laid on this plate, put into a press and immediately the design is transferred onto the paper and allowed to dry. Finally it is coloured by hand. Once the engraved plate had been made there was really no limit to the number of leaves which could be produced cheaply and quickly, cheaply enough for them to be ripped from their very simple sticks when a new one emerged – 'off with the old, on with the new'! These fan leaves, hot from the press, were easily mounted and, when printed in numbers, cost as little as two shillings each. In some cases only a few were prepared, in other cases there were hundreds. It was said that during the nineteenth century there were upwards of one thousand different printed fans in Europe portraying Napoleon and his exploits.

Mass-production has naturally meant that etched fans are neither especially artistic nor very valuable, but it did bring the fan on to the horizon of the woman who was a little less wealthy, and has produced fans that have historical interest.

Printed fans depicted a whole variety of topics, and most of them are great fun; there were maps of counties such as Warwickshire or Dorset; perpetual almanacks; those showing the building and maps of the Nicaragua Canal and the canal in Madrid; quizzes; games like 'snakes and ladders' but with careers; riddles; conundrums as poor as those still found in Christmas crackers; and even a punning Bill of Fare for a wedding

dinner in 1794 with dishes labelled 'Part of the Zodiac, buttered' or 'A Blockhead hashed' and even 'Melancholy Soup with Crooked Sauce'.

Amongst the most popular topics for celebrating, or mourning, were events from contemporary history: an early fan shows the coronation banquet of George II in 1727; another depicts Queen Anne's wedding (fig. 70); another shows Admiral Vernon after his victory at Porto Bello in 1739; one depicts the trial of Warren Hastings in 1788; endless fans showing the Peninsular Wars, with or without Wellington; just as many show Napoleon, in or out of Russia, wreathed in

laurel leaves as usual; there is a salute to the building of the Statue of Liberty (a gift from France) and many charming ones which were rather more personal.

Printed fans provide the most wonderful means to see what people really felt or did or wore at a given moment. They have immense vitality because it is only too obvious that they were entirely 'of their time', and they give the viewer the opportunity to look into people's lives and thoughts just as though he was looking through a window. Of the many fan leaves one sees, most are memorable because they give an extra insight into life in those days, and several of these have an extra curiosity value in themselves. Take, for instance, a fan leaf in the Schrieber Collection in the British Museum—an excellent collection with an invaluable catalogue—called 'The Honours in Cards' and showing the various suits, hearts, spades, diamonds and clubs, with poems relating to each. We all know 'The Queen of Hearts, she made some tarts . . .' but how many of us know the other suits? What about:

> The Diamond Queen
> Was one day seen
> So drunk she could not stand.
> The Diamond Knave
> He blush'd and gave
> The Queen a reprimand.
> The King, distress'd
> That his Dearest
> Should do so vile a thing
> Said 'By my wig
> She's like the pig
> Of David the good King.'

Apparently the lust-for-life Georgians revelled in that type of thing but the Victorians must conveniently have let that part of the sequence drop.

One of the earliest printed fans in the Schrieber Collection was called 'Mr. Thomas Osborne's Duck Hunting 1754', the leaf being etched, coloured by hand and mounted on wooden sticks. Looking at the detail is as good as reading a tapestry sequence in medieval days or watching a cartoon by Walt Disney. The story behind this fan is amusing and fortunately Mr Thomas Osborne's daughter wrote an account of what happened to clear up the details for us. She says:

'Mr. Thomas Osborne, or, as he was more commonly called, Tommy Osborne, was a very considerable book-seller and publisher in Gray's Inn, Holborn. He bought the Harleian Collection of printed books, and published a sale catalogue.

Dr. Samuel Johnson has been said to be the compiler of this catalogue. In 1754 he had a house at Hampstead, which was then a watering place. A Captain Pratten constituted himself Master of Ceremonies at the Assembly Rooms. Among the fixed residents was a Mr. Scarlet, a celebrated optician. Captain Pratten was more particular in his attentions to Mrs. Scarlet than to any other lady, and was her inseparate companion in her walks and visits. As Mrs. Scarlet was remarkably plain in the person, the voice of scandal declared that this attention was repaid by the use of her purse. When Mr. Osborne settled himself in his new house, Captain Pratten proposed to him that he should ingratiate himself with the families of Hampstead by giving a public breakfast for the ladies, and a duck hunting for the gentlemen.

'Tommy Osborne, though very successful in business, was not esteemed very acute in private, and fell into the scheme, and left the whole management to Captain Pratten. Invitations were sent to all the genteel families in the place, and marquees erected for the breakfast, and ducks were provided for the hunting. The company assembled, and were so happy that they were loath to depart. Captain Pratten was everywhere, and, finding things went so merrily, suggested to Mr. Osborne that he had better continue the entertainment with a cold collation.

'Still the company lingered, and Captain Pratten and Mrs. Scarlet circulated in whispers that if they stayed they would have a dance to conclude the day. The whole company took the hint, smiling at their host's vanity and expense. The long dancing tents were put up in the courtyard, and the younger part of the company tripped the light fantastic toe till bedtime. To prolong the memory of this day of enjoyment, Captain Pratten

72   *Two fans.* Top *printed and hand-coloured fan of political subject, probably the capture of Porto Bello by Admiral Vernon in 1739. Dated 1740, signed S. Clark. By courtesy of the Countess of Rosse. Messell Collection. Bottom printed and hand-coloured fan, scene from a play or opera. Ivory painted sticks, dated 1740. By courtesy of the Countess of Rosse. Messell Collection*

further persuaded Mr. Osborne to have a fan engraved and presented to each of his lady visitors.'

The amiable and gullible Mr Osborne did as Captain Pratten advised and these commemorative fans showing absolutely everything from ducks to dancing tents and a very elegant parade of ladies and gentlemen.

There seem to be almost no limits on the subjects printed fans covered from political cartoons to scenes from books (see fig. 73) or gipsy fortune-telling. Plays were advertised and so were watering-places and coach time-tables; important events were celebrated such as King George III's recovery from insanity (it was temporary) which, to quote the caption on the fan 'brought health to one and happiness to millions'.

Their advertising potential was exploited by those sharp enough to put scenes from plays on fans, or scenes from operas, such as

Nina or *The Marriage of Figaro*, with a snatch of music round the sides. Almost all printed fan leaves in England have their date of issue on them, together with the name of the publishers, in accordance with the provisions of an Act of 1735. When dates are missing it was not because of cheating but because they were cut off to fit the leaf onto the sticks. Especially worth looking out for are those printed by Mr Gamble 'at the Sign of the Golden Fan' during the mid-eighteenth century.

During the Neo-classical period naturally a very great many printed and etched fans were made (fig. 71). Their colours were chosen to match clothes.

Fans were even made for the care of one's soul, with the Church fans and the Chapel fans (figs. 74 and 75). Quite often a series of these were left at the porch for the congregation to help themselves on a sultry hot day when the sermon threatened to last two hours. The differences between the two tell us something about the denominations. The Church fan gives prayers, the Ten Commandments, and the Creed. The Chapel fan gives Psalms and 'An example of Thrift', and leaves out a prayer to the Royal Family which Church-goers had to repeat.

Fans provided, too, for one's entertainment, with numerous dance fans which showed the latest music and dance-steps; in a dance fan for 1798 there were twenty dances enumerated and described, including 'Taffy's Fancy' and 'The Marquis of Huntley's Highland Fling'. By now people were dancing together, man and woman. This was considered extremely daring behaviour, just as seating a man between two women at a dinner party was considered scandalous and called 'promiscuous seating'.

Towards the end of the century the design and the colours of a fan came to be an indication of the politics of the holder. In the days before mass literacy one way of indicating your politics was through the dress you wore, perhaps sporting some particular colour scheme or special garment. For instance, the patriotic Frenchman of 1789 was an incarnation of the tricolour; blue was the colour of Liberty, white of Equality and red of Fraternity; and naturally he would wear his revolutionary Phrygian or 'galley-slave' cap as well. But people did not have to create an impression deliberately for one to be inferred. One parodist saw the birth of a new political movement in Ireland through the dress of the people:

Their hats caved in and shapeless to
        slight the Crown are meant,
Their knickerbockers and gaiters show a
        desperate attempt,
Their beards look all seditious from the
        tips unto the roots,
But there's mischief *beyond measure* in
        their square-toed boots.

Hats and boots were, above every other

73 *English late 18th century etched fan showing scenes from Sterne's* Sentimental Journey. *Victoria and Albert Museum, Crown copyright*

article of dress, the most frequently chosen as means of showing political feelings, and for women fans came a close third.

In England the state of politics was not as desperate as in Ireland or France, publicity was not so pressing, and soon fan-making almost died out altogether. In the year 1822 there were only nine names of London fan-makers recorded and in 1839 the number was down to two. Yet in other European countries they were still being made, but reverting from both the painted fan and the printed fan to those made from textiles or feathers.

France

The French Revolution gave the manufacture of printed fans an enormous impetus with satires, homilies and declarations covered with emblems, political sentiments and like-nesses of popular leaders printed directly onto paper or even cut out to be pasted onto muslin or wood.

Revolutions always make a difference to manner and modes. It would have been madness for someone to carry a jewelled fan in the streets after the French Revolution, yet fashionable women still had to carry *something*. Fashions had now all changed to Republican styles. White, gold and purple were the colours of Republican Rome so they were seen all over Europe in dress for at least twenty years; textiles changed from brocades to muslins, batistes and embroidered Indian cottons. The hoop was abandoned as the flimsy materials clung, sometimes with the surreptitious aid of a good dousing of water, to the hitherto unseen figure. Breasts had been observed with interest for years and years but the hips and legs were altogether new and exciting. Every lady now attempted to look like a Greek goddess, or Greek at any rate, but they simply could not bear to let go of their fans. Even Charlotte Corday,

74 *A Chapel fan, English, dated 1796. The mount engraved, the sticks of wood. Victoria and Albert Museum, Crown Copyright*

75 *A Church fan, English, dated 1796. The mount engraved, the sticks of ivory. Victoria and Albert Museum, Crown copyright*

76 *The Madonna of Loretto fan,
French, early 19th century. This
fan commemorates the capture of
the Madonna of Loretto by
Napoleon from Rome. The case
in which the statue was
transported can be seen on the
left. Its mount is engraved; the
sticks are of ivory; the guards
have silver piqué. Victoria and
Albert Museum, Crown
copyright*

as she stabbed Marat in his bath (he had
an unfortunate skin-disease that only warm
baths could alleviate) held her fan firmly in
her other hand – a matter which caused a
good deal of interest when it came out at her
trial.

Women also took to using constitutional
fans to show their sympathies, showing the
articles of their new Constitution or the
Tricolour, or fans that proclaimed 'Liberté,
Egalité, Fraternité', and even some with
portraits of French Republican officials. When
Charlotte Corday reached her moment of
triumph it was a Constitutional fan she was
holding.

Fans were, in fact, political rather than pure

fashion objects. Commemorative fans had been extraordinarily popular during the late eighteenth century. Many show such scenes as General Wolfe at Quebec or the death of Mirabeau in 1791; Marie Antoinette was given a perpetual almanack on a fan in 1771 and there was also the 'Death of Lincoln' in the United States and 'The Meeting of the Estates General' in 1789. In 1794, of the 200 engravings which were lodged in the Bibliothèque Nationale during the year (and this was their finest political outlet), 114 were political fan designs. They were not beautiful; fans had shed their expensive decoration, and, no longer having to balance the width of a crinoline or a towering coiffure, they had shrunk in size. Nor could they compete with the marvellously enriched sticks and guards of the earlier fans. The beautiful painted fan, so much admired during the early and middle years of the eighteenth century, was now a thing of the past, and, by 1806, hardly a fan of any type is mentioned in reports of the fashions of society.

Most of these printed fans were in black or sanguine and over-coloured by hand. They were eventually overtaken by the lithographed fan (the invention was in 1798) which was also hand-coloured but at its most popular during the 1840s, unfortunately mainly brassily over-gilded on the florid colouring. Care must be taken to distinguish between printed leaves, lithographed leaves and those which have pen and ink drawings, lightly over-coloured and often used for mourning fans.

For a while fans were very small and made of textiles and then the fashion for them revived during the mid-nineteenth century. But painted fans and especially those from rich-looking textiles, feathers and lace took the place of the slightly austere printed fan and they were eventually seen no more.

The ballooning fan

One attractive use of the printed fan which is

Overleaf
77 Top *The NADFAS fan, English, 18th century.*

Bottom
German or English folding fan, c.1730. The mount is of pleated paper showing a scene at the races with jockeys on horseback together with mounted spectators, both men and women, quite possibly the first races seen at Ascot. The sticks of tortoiseshell, the guards having a narrow triangular shape with rounded shoulders and carved at the top with a spray of flowers. Victoria and Albert Museum, Crown copyright

78 Top *Chinese fixed fan 19th century. This racquet-shaped fan was never designed to fold. A colourfully enamelled handle which imitates bamboo is attached to a mount framed in tortoiseshell over which gilt thread gauze is stretched. An appliqué design is applied of embroidered silk with an enamelled plaque which represents a floral palmette. There are twin tassels and an elaborate knob.*

Bottom
Chinese ivory brisé circular fan, first half of the 18th century. This tiny fan is designed with seven cartouches, the sticks are minutely carved with buds and flowers and have circular loop ends; the whole held together with a striped silk ribbon. Victoria and Albert Museum, Crown copyright

not political is the advent of the ballooning fan or the *Montgolfières*. The early history of ballooning is, astonishingly, recorded in about 500 prints. Many are hand-coloured, and they show both types of balloons: the 'hot-air' balloon invented by Joseph and Étienne Montgolfier in 1782 and the hydrogen balloon invented by Professor Charles in 1783. As the entire success of printing depends upon the paper manufacturers and the publishers it comes as no surprise that so much publicity was given to the balloon ascents by the Brothers Montgolfier, paper manufacturers from near Lyons. Ascents from balloons were thrilling people in most of the European countries, but frightening people in others to the extent that they shot at Professor Charles's first unmanned balloon when it came down and attacked it with pitchforks (they thought it carried creatures from outer space).

The first balloons were filled with livestock, as it seemed safer, and anyway the French

Right
79 Printed and hand-coloured paper fan, European, japanned wooden sticks. Inscribed 'Bosselman Sculpt.', c.1820-30. The artist here has attempted to return to the spacious composition of mid 18th century fans. By courtesy of the Countess of Rosse, Messell Collection

80 Montgolfière fan, French, late 18th century, with silvered ivory stick and guards and paste stud. Rijksmuseum, Amsterdam

have never been as sentimental about animals as the English, so a cock, a sheep and a duck went up, and, luckily, came down again eight minutes later.

Then the daring experiment was made to give a balloon a human pilot, J. F. Pilâtre de Rozier (1756-85), who flew happily about for twenty-five minutes; but it was Jean-Pierre Blanchard (1753-1809) who was the first professional balloonist, making over sixty ascents. An exceedingly brave husband and wife were the first people ever to make descents by parachute, André Jacques Garnerin (1769-1825) and his wife Jeanne Geneviève (1779-1847), going up in their balloons and sitting for a while in the most elaborate boat-shaped baskets before they floated down again.

The balloons were a glorious sight, far more colourful than the two tiny ones seen in fig. 80 and the other on the silvered ivory sticks. They were coloured with circles and stripes, pinks, whites and blues, even a Union Jack all over the balloon which made the first ascent in England by Vincent Lunardi in 1784, and the boat-shaped baskets were painted to match or to contrast and national flags hung fore and aft. They were obviously a perfect subject for a printed fan.

It is as well to look out for them. There are at least ten different examples known, four in the Schrieber Collection, and amusing to judge for yourself whether the balloon is hot-air or hydrogen, as well as pin-pointing the personalities and the actual event.

Today there is a select band of people who collect, most profitably, ballooning prints; some of the originals can be seen in the collections of aero clubs in England, France and the United States or in national patent offices, and it is a great addition to a fan collection to have a ballooning fan.

Oriental fans

The customs of using fans in the Orient are legion and started before written records both in China and Japan. However, it is known that they were used, at every gradation on the social scale, from the Mikado (emperor), who was revered as a living god by all Japanese, to the common labourer. Whether he sat swathed in silken robes and sitting in silent state upon his throne, or whether he wore his loose blue robes as a working man, a person from whatever class, man or woman, court official, sage, priest, prince or nobleman, dancing-girl or child would own a fan as part of his birth-right. The differences between the social ranks were precise and un-questioned, reaching down to every detail of life, and even fans were made of a particular design according to rank, position or pro-fession, and would remain unchanged from generation to generation.

A very strict code concerning the in-dividual use of each fan was established, as strict as the etiquette of the court of Louis XIV. Manners decreed that, when out walking, the fan could be held open; indoors it was the rule to slip it in the *obi* (or sash) or to dispose of it in the sleeve. Should one have a guest, as soon as he was seated on the floor the fan might be removed and placed either in front of or on the left hand side of him; he might then take it up once or twice, half-open it or toy with it, but never use it for real fanning unless he was amongst the most intimate of friends.

Another small point of etiquette in the home was the banning of the use of a fan in the presence of carefully arranged flowers. This was considered very bad form indeed, for flower-arranging was a meticulous art which took a long time.

Because its use was symbolic the occasions for which a fan would be made were myriad: for a coming-of-age at sixteen for instance, a marriage gift, a first-interview present and a present from a bride to her groom (she had to bring seven gifts to him, one of which had to be a fan), for jugglers or ringers, as maps and newspapers before they became com-mon, and for the tea ceremonies. A priest would use a fan to make a point in a sermon; in his temple he found his hands occupied when carrying food to the god so he folded his fan and slid it in his gown behind his neck, but when he prayed he held up his fan with both hands and raised it towards his head as he bowed. Also, as the decorations on Japanese fans were based upon the symbols of a prosperous life, unity and good fortune, they were all seen in the traditional ceremony at the completion of a building when the 'Fan House Emblem' was set upon the finished roof; this consisted of three fans with a metal mirror fixed into the centre, a long lock of a woman's hair and a perch (*tai*) in a dish.

The fans of the emperors of Japan have

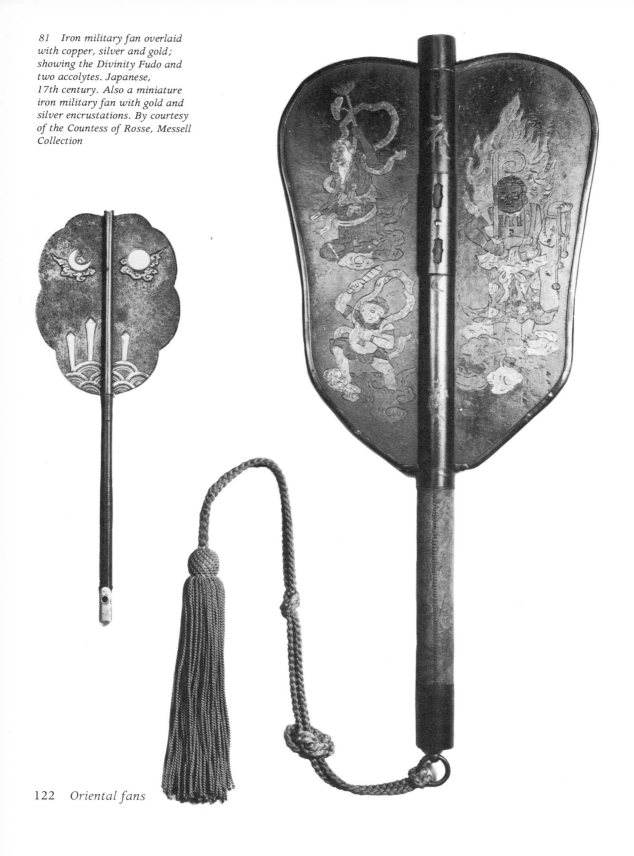

81 Iron military fan overlaid
with copper, silver and gold;
showing the Divinity Fudo and
two accolytes. Japanese,
17th century. Also a miniature
iron military fan with gold and
silver encrustations. By courtesy
of the Countess of Rosse, Messell
Collection

been recorded since the Emperor Gosanjo (reigned 1068-72) had a folding fan which needed repairing. In the Treasury of the Temple of Itsukushima there are some very historic fans deposited and fully authenticated, including one of which belonged to the young Emperor Antoku, who was drowned at the Battle of Dan-no-ura in 1185, aged six. This little fan (only 16 cm., $6\frac{1}{4}$ in. long) is made of thirty-nine blades of wood covered over with small landscape sketches which show a great many tiny little figures. It is strung together at the top and has an ornamental rivet-head.

The first few lay Europeans who came to Japan were the merchant adventurers of the sixteenth and seventeenth centuries, mainly the Dutch. They were largely devoid of culture or any real interest in the strange new world of the Japanese; the Shōgun and samurai (military class) despised them as tradesmen and it is therefore extremely rare to find arms and military objects such as battle fans decorated with European subjects. However, it is possible, though most unusual, to pick up an eighteenth-century Japanese fan with the impression 'V.O.C.', for this was the emblem of the Dutch East India Company, Vereenighde Oostindische Compagnie, the only traders who were permitted to enter any of Japan's ports and who imported into Europe some of the artistic treasures of the Far East. Then Japan was largely shut off from the rest of the world. She had a dual form of government which dated back to the eleventh century. The country's titular and religious head was the Mikado, or emperor, while the secular and administrative power resided with the military leader, the Shōgun. Then, in 1868 the Mikado defeated the Shōgun after much internal struggling and became absolute ruler. At this time, through considerable pressure applied by the Americans, who sent an envoy in the person of Commodore Perry, gradually the Japanese began to open their doors to the outside world. France immediately poured in money to help

them with their considerable programme of building ship-yards, docks, iron-foundries, etc. and accepted as a return their works of art.

After the Mikado put down the Shōgun the feudal system was abolished. The Daimos, or princes of allotted provinces, laid down their swords (some willingly, some more reluctantly) and the more advanced patriots began to long for an interchange of thought and speech with foreigners. From this time onwards Japan has changed, virtually for the first time only, and it is only in the last quarter century that her people have come into line with the dress and social customs of most of the rest of the world. Nowadays only a few men and women wear the kimono and carry their own particular type of fan, the emperor is no longer considered officially a god and the wealthy merchant plays golf. This means that fans are rarely used and some of those that were in currency are now available for the interested collector. But the collector would be wise to try and distinguish between the types, for they vary more than in any other country.

Types and shapes

There are two basic types of fan in the Orient, called in Japan the *uchiwa*, which are rigid flat fans, and the *ogi* or *sensu*, meaning the folding fans. The *uchiwa* can be beautifully decorated but more often fulfil simple and useful functions such as kitchen bellows. The *ogi* were originally used at court, by aristocrats. One pastime, called *ogi-nagashi*, was popular with aristocratic ladies for many years. It is reported to have begun when Emperor Higashiyama (1688-1710) went to Saga and held a boating excursion on the River Oi. One of the ladies accidentally dropped her fan into the water and it floated down the river, making such a pretty picture that the other ladies followed her example. Fan-floating, which is how *ogi-nagashi* translates, soon became a leisurely game.

The fans of Japanese empresses were made of twenty-three blades of cyprus wood painted with flowers, in combinations which were used exclusively by them: the chrysanthemum, the pine-tree, orange-blossom, plum or camellia japonica. Their most outstanding features were the silks and the tassels. Their blades were held with a coloured silk and where these fastening ribbons ended there were tassels fixed, all of 125 cm. (4 ft.) long, consisting of seven silk cords of seven colours ornamentally knotted to match the floral decorations on the blades; and the rivet was exclusively paper string.

Ribbon streamers, silken tassels and ornamental knots have always been an important part of the Japanese fan, later on, when one or two were seen in France during the seventeenth century the Lyons centre of silk and ribbon-making took up this idea enthusiastically, to such an extent that the eighteenth-century is often known as 'the ribbon era' in dress, jewellery, painted decorations on walls and ceilings and in ceramics.

An open court fan carried until the defeat of the Shōgun (in use since the seventh century), known as the *Akome ogi*, was made of thirty-nine blades of wood painted white, decorated with cherry, pine, plum or chrysanthemums on gold or silver powder 'amongst the mist' or set within clouds. The rivet was formed like a bird or a butterfly and it was ornamented at the corners with hanging clusters of artificial flowers made of silk and two silk tassels. Each twist of the tassels consisted of twelve strands of different coloured silks, and the knots were very often made into the shape of a family crest, such as the wisteria for the Fujiwara families. Sometimes carved ivory balls were attached by tassels.

Another form of court fan was the *komori*, named after the bat (see p. 12). The frame was made of fourteen bamboo sticks and the leaf of paper, coloured gold, silver, red, purple, blue, yellow or white but never, on any account, the unlucky colours of green or light purple. These fans looked as though they were partially open even when firmly closed because of a flexible joint in the outside frame. It is also interesting to note how often the outer sticks or guards in Japanese fans extend slightly beyond the top of the leaf and are shaped to curve inwards a little in order to close more firmly. One of the most interesting types of fan in the Orient is the one carried by the commander in battle and often made of iron, to be used for giving directions and, if need be, as a weapon (fig. 81). These metal fans are very heavy. A smaller, miniature one on the left in the illustration, probably made for the Boys' Festival, is also made of iron with gold and silver encrustations, showing the sun and the moon above the sea and rocks.

Sometimes the commander's fan was made of a combination of metal, paper and leather. One exhibited in the Liverpool Art Club exhibition of 1877 is described in the catalogue:

'The leaf is of stout buff paper, covered with silk tissue, painted on the front with a group of figures, the Seven Sages in the Forest of Bamborn, chiefly in Indian ink, and drawn with great spirit; and on the back with temple, buildings and foliage. The sticks are plain whalebone; but the most interesting and remarkable portions of the fan are the guards, which are of oxidised iron elaborately inlaid with scroll-work and crests in silver, the crests are those of the powerful family of Nai-To. The handle is of leather.'

Another use for a fan which is totally authoritarian is that which is carried by the Japanese umpire at wrestling (*sumo*) matches. It is sturdily and heavily made as a fiddle or pear-shape with two wings. The handle comes right down through the middle of the leaf, dividing it into two parts (very much

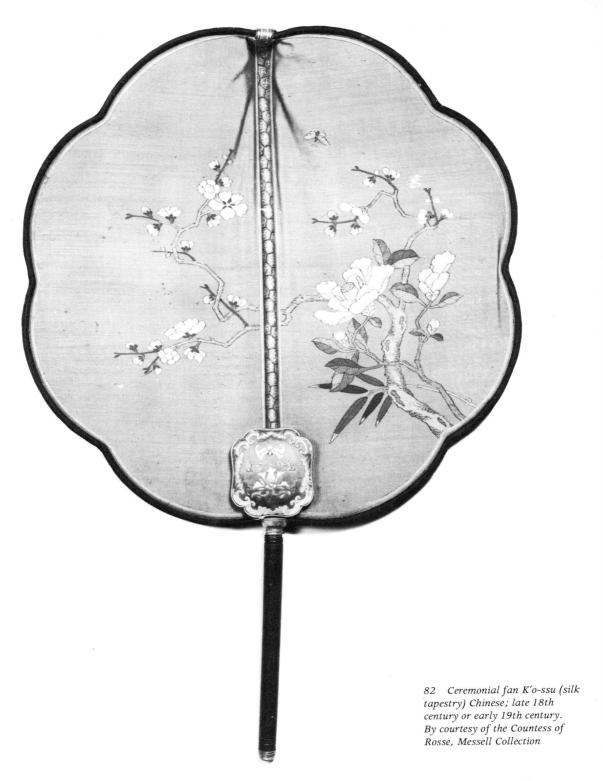

82 Ceremonial fan K'o-ssu (silk
tapestry) Chinese; late 18th
century or early 19th century.
By courtesy of the Countess of
Rosse, Messell Collection

Oriental fans 125

like the battle fan already mentioned in fig. 81) and sometimes the words 'one mind, one voice' are painted on it to show that the umpire's decision was binding, as it unquestionably was, and is today.

Oriental artists are passionately interested in the effects of light. Some of their fans bear identical pictures, one on each side. These are painted not too elaborately and with plenty of spare background space. One of the pictures is the reverse of the other, so when the fan, which is made of a semi-transparent material or paper, is held up to the light, there is a magical effect of looking at an image and its shadow.

Another fan on the same style has two sheets of material or fine-grade paper, again semi-transparent, with absolutely nothing painted on them but an emblem (a crab, a butterfly, or a part of a family's coat of arms) fixed between the two sheets. When held down the fan looks quite plain and simple, when held against the light the ghost or spirit of a crab or butterfly appears caught in the meshes of the fan. The first of these appeared in the province of Yamato around the year 1800 and they are called *Yamato* fans as a result.

In China they used to make hand-screens on exactly the same lines with embroidered materials such as gauze, one side in reverse to the other. In the collection of the late Queen Mary there was a beautiful pair of these embroidered translucent hand-screens, and sometimes they can be acquired today, still in very good condition. In fig. 82 there is a beautiful ceremonial fan of silk tapestry (K'o-ssu) from China of the late eighteenth or early nineteenth century with the most delicate of embroideries.

Among the most romantic Oriental fans are those seen in the Japanese Noh theatre, the traditional and unchanging drama that dates back to the Middle Ages. The Noh dramas represent a blending of folk and temple dances which achieved their present form about 600 years ago. They are a balance of dance and music combined with drama, almost exclusively an aristocratic art form, and all but incomprehensible. Over the years commoners were forbidden to attend or to create their own performances and the Noh dramas became so exclusive that the plays were given in specially constructed theatres, and actors were rewarded with samurai rank to enable them to perform at all. The Noh dedicated itself to constancy: the speech, the music, the dance and the dress are traditional – and this atmosphere of sequestered exclusiveness perhaps explains the anonymity of the artists who painted their fans and the difficulties of dating them with any real accuracy. The painters were content to create merely under court patronage and each generation of painters sought to work within the old traditions rather than to find new methods of expression. It is said that much that is characteristic of the Noh is revealed in the fan-painting; the stage itself is simple and stark but the costumes are brilliant to the point of flamboyancy, this gorgeousness being shared by the fans. Symbolism permeates the drama as it does the paintings. Such subjects as ancient pines, cherry blossoms, dragons, pheasants, the phoenix, maples in Autumn and so on were charged with particular meanings for a Japanese audience, who would be completely in tune with such phrases painted on a fan as, 'After a thousand years even the fir-tree must pass away'.

So widespread was the fan in the Orient that it was customary politeness to have special fans to offer guests on arrival. These were of a very high quality of craftsmanship and decoration. They were always available and were placed upon a fan rack in the living area of a house. It is possible to find these old fan racks on occasion and they make an interesting addition to a fan collection. They were generally made of the large type of bamboo, split in half and decorated. They have a series of double hooks, sometimes of silver, on which to rest the fans; and a fitment at the top, sometimes merely a hole, with which they can be hung up against the pillars of the room. Some are quite beautifully carved, in wood or raised lacquer. One seventeenth-century lacquer artist, Ritsuo, in particular was famed for his fan racks, and it would be well worth looking out for fan-racks in the future (if you do not own one already) for many people are simply unaware what they are supposed to be.

Painted fans

Painting fan leaves has always been regarded as a branch of the Fine Arts in the Orient, from the first painted fan in the Sung Dynasty onwards. Many have been carefully stored in albums rather than put to practical use as they were considered too precious. In Europe rich patrons have always collected easel paintings; in the East they collected *kake-mono* (scroll paintings) and fan leaves, not only the original masterpieces but copies of them by other fine artists, even permutations and combinations of the masterpieces as well. In the past they have rarely been for sale outside the East where their owners guarded them closely, yet a collection of fans would be totally incomplete without a Japanese or Chinese painted or printed fan, and now that their art is circulating more freely it should be more likely that an Oriental fan-leaf or fan will come your way.

Chinese and Japanese art is extremely difficult for the average Western mind to understand because we look at Western art from a totally different point of view. Approaching Oriental art with any pre-conceived ideas is a complete mistake and the more one knows about Western art the less easy it is to understand Oriental art. There are two things that one could do, either abandon all attempts to get to grips with the subject and leave it severely alone, or start from the beginning.

In the West the person interested in paintings goes to an exhibition and immediately asks various questions such as, 'Who painted this? What is its date? What is its style? What does it mean to me? How good is it?'; yet when the same person is confronted with an Oriental painting he or she is generally quite lost and is filled with a depressing feeling of inadequacy. The majority of people cannot say with any confidence whether the painting is good or bad, old or new, an original or a copy or, even worse, whether it is Chinese or Japanese.

It is not the viewer's fault; there are very few books, which are largely inaccessible anyway, written in English on the subject which set out the principles clearly and concisely from the Western point of view. Universities and museums are very diffident when answering queries and give innumerable qualifications to their answers – far better, however, than the so-called 'expert' who gives a quick and confident judgement which one should view with the utmost suspicion.

The matter becomes even more difficult when one realizes that most of the recent judgements on Chinese art available to us in written form have been produced by the Japanese, although perhaps with the gradual opening-up of Chinese boundaries we may eventually be able to see the Chinese art-historians' own evaluations. This explains why so many Chinese works of art are mistaken for Japanese rather than the other way about, and why Japanese terms are used such as *kakemono* for Chinese scrolls or *sansui* for Chinese landscapes. It is all very confusing.

Many people in the West, though not painters themselves, feel quite capable of judging the quality of a picture, simply because a sound knowledge of painting techniques is not a prerequisite of authoritative criticism. This could not be so in the East, there a working knowledge of techniques is absolutely essential; there the understanding and enjoyment of painting is by knowing how it is done, why it is done and what it means when it is done in a certain format. Once this is understood it is possible to make a start in understanding, appreciating, and loving the elusive beauty, strange and eternally intangible of Chinese and Japanese art. In the West painting techniques have always been regarded as more or less the hand-maiden of an idea, so they could be deposed as being of secondary importance, but in the East techniques are completely inseparable from the philosophy behind the painting, leading one's mind thereby into deep and serious thoughts and contemplative ideals.

We find as well that in the East magic and philosophy were always indivisible, and in a world dominated by the supernatural people could not possibly conceive of the brush-stroke and the idea as being two distinct things, nor as existing on different levels, nor as representing the opposite poles of the material and the spiritual. Western philosophy is primarily dualistic, separating and opposing the material and the spiritual, and magic is regarded as little more than a joke. In the East, certainly until the beginning of this century, almost everyone believed in certain forms of magic and no-one laughed at them for so doing. Magic, in the East, is seen as an essential part of art – magic, after all, is in one's imagination and so much in Oriental art is left to one's own imaginative interpretation. A famous Chinese tale illustrates the Chinese attitude to the magic in art:

There was once a great emperor who asked the most wonderful artist in his country, Wu Tao-tzu, to paint a landscape for him on the palace wall. Wu set to work and eventually finished his masterpiece, leading the emperor up to a magnificent landscape into whose centre he had painted a dark and mysterious cave. The emperor was astonished at the lifelike quality of the work and was expressing his admiration to the courtiers about him when Wu walked away from him towards the painting, walked up to the cave and right inside it; just as his body disappeared from sight the entire painting gathered itself up and disappeared into the palace wall as well, leaving it quite blank again.

It has always been a tradition in Japan as well that painters accomplished miracles on fans in earlier epochs; one account tells of Tadahira, who is said to have painted on a fan a cuckoo so lifelike that every time it was opened it sang its characteristic song; and another tells of Tsunenori, who drew such a lifelike lion on a fan that all other animals ran away at the sight of it.

The Oriental mind finds this eminently understandable. Very great artists have a quality of magic about them that is perfectly acceptable. Just as we in the West speak of genius, so they in the East speak about magic. But their artists only acquire that magic after years of apprenticeship and practice; ability could be innate, magic comes from years of hard work, the stages of which were most carefully laid down. The Oriental mind loves to catalogue, to systematize, always on the basis of tried and true and recognized maxims.

It is this quality of recognized rules and regulations that makes identifying paintings on fans easier for the Westerner, and if a few of the following guide-lines are borne in mind by the fan-collector a whole new world opens up as Chinese or Japanese fans are added to a collection.

That painted fans from Europe should be considered the finest is a mistake. They are in a category of their own and their crafts-manship as a whole should be recognized rather than their great painterly quality. On the other hand, many fans from Japan are real works of art by the recognized best painters of their period created for their own people; the curious ones are those which were made for the export market.

Very deep thought was given to the laws of proportion and design. First consideration was the space and shape available, then the distribution of light and shade and finally the harmonious placing of the painted scene on the scroll, fan, or screen.

To a certain extent screen-painting is the parent to fan-painting; both have a great deal in common and fans which were used in the home were made to harmonize with the screens. There used to be screens in ancient China and Korea and the Japanese adopted the use of paper hinged-screens from them, making screen-painting essentially a Japanese art by developing the conception of a pair of screens with a right-handed and a left-handed composition. This created a single complete design, bringing balance and harmony into a room, and then the painting of a fan to be used in this room would have some element of the design as its decoration. They never made the mistake of trying to paint the whole composition across the fan in miniature, but they just took a flower, maybe, or a butterfly within leaves out of the composition and reproduced it upon the fan in order to carry the subtle harmonies even further.

The paintings on screens and fans during the Fujiwara period (897-1185) showed religious designs, those of the Ashikaga period (1392-1568) were mainly domestic, those of the Momoyama (1568-1615) were the most brilliant of all with gold leaf inlaid, a huge range of zinging colours and corresponding in Oriental art with the High Renaissance in Italy. Within and across the styles of the periods, there are also distinctive schools.

Japanese schools

During the long and peaceful time from the Edo period to the Restoration (1615-1867) the Japanese were left in tranquility to develop their own art forms; the country was closed to trade and the outer world, the people learnt to relax in a period of deep peace and their arts and crafts flourished and developed undisturbed. Most of their best fans were created at this time.

During the fifteenth century the Chinese influenced the Japanese painters enormously and among the schools which flourished at that time in Japan one stood out further than the rest, the Kanō School. The Kanō School eventually had a very far-reaching and persistent influence which, through a line of brilliant artists, handed down its great traditions to many artists of the twentieth century. The leadership descended in both the great Schools of Kanō and Tosa in family succession from one generation to another in a proper feudal style; the first master of the Kanō School (and a member of the famous Fujiwara family) was Kanō Masanobu (c. 1424-1520). During his period the style was characterized by a monochrome brilliance and apparent swiftness of the brush; later the Kanō School brought in a huge richness of colour, a pronounced decorative effect by its intricacy of design. It was they who introduced a completely new style of rich colours on a gold ground, and in figs. 84 and 85 one can see two fan leaves in the two distinct styles. Although of the seventeenth century fig. 84 shows the earlier style of painting with what appears to be the lightest of brush-strokes and tonal nuances in *sumi* (the technique is explained on page 141); fig. 85 has the brilliant colours of the later style.

The Kanō school also introduced new subjects to add to the old traditional mono-chromatic scenes of landscapes or aspects of nature. They painted episodes from court life, foreigners, missionaries or merchants, and mythological themes, using superlative brush technique. Because they were especially favoured by the Shōguns of the Tokugawa period (1615-1867) the teachings of Kanō artists were quickly spread throughout Japan. Many of the artists who created independent styles were taught at first in Kanō studios or assimilated the Kanō standards first hand, and continued to do so right up to the end of the nineteenth century.

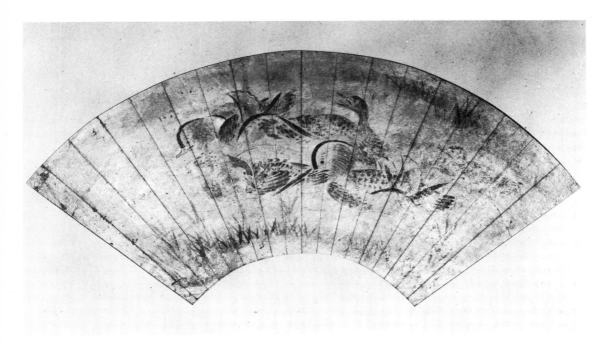

84 *Painted fan leaf, showing mandarin ducks, symbolic of married happiness. Japanese, Kanō School, 17th-18th centuries. By courtesy of the Countess of Rosse, Messell Collection*

The Tosa school was traditionally supported by the court circle, as opposed to the Kanō school and their Shōgun patronage. Their work is the most typically Japanese and is concerned with subjects from Japanese history and literature. It is based on traditional Yamato-e painting and illustration and can be recognized by its wiry line and minute presentation of details.

There are four illustrations here from the Tosa school, figs. 83, 86, 87 and 88 showing scenes from everyday Japanese court life from the serene parade of court ladies in fig. 83, via the armed nobleman on horseback to the two dancers pirouetting in the Bugaku dance and finally to the most curious and original perspective in fig. 88. Opening up the building to view the rooms and terraces is typical of this style, the artist has 'thought' them away and left the subject totally unconcerned in his architectural nakedness. An off-shoot of the Kanō school was the Kōrin school where the artists were known to use powdered gold or precious stones in their pigments, giving them a special form of brilliance, although in fig. 90 the subject of an *onaga-dori* (a small, long-tailed bird) and chrysanthemums (for purity) does not show this here. The school was begun by Ogata Kōrin (1658-1716) with wonderful rhythmic patterning and the framed brilliant colours which, according to Therle Hughes in *Country Life*, June 1972, '. . . might be

85 Painted fan leaf showing
Kinko, a mythological figure,
riding on a carp. Japanese, Kanō
School, 17th-18th centuries.
By courtesy of the Countess of
Rosse, Messel Collection

expected from the son of a great brocade merchant'.

The Shijō school, which derived from the naturalistic painter Maruyama Ōkyo (1733-95), flourished in Kyoto from the latter part of the eighteenth century and was founded by the artist Matsumura Goshun (1752-1811). There is a very charming illustration of the work of Kwaito from this School in fig. 91, showing a sparrow with a grasshopper and dated *Kanobo-Hitsuji*, which probably corresponds with the year 1811.

Each great school has influenced the others at certain periods and their emergence accompanied the spread of education as well as the increasing wealth of the merchants during the Tokugawa period, existing so peacefully as they drifted on the tide of insularity away from the world. Between them all they painted some great masterpieces on fans, scrolls and screens.

During the eighteenth century there was another school, the plebian Ukijo-e (or 'floating world' school) of Edo. These artists did not paint serious or traditional scenes of sages and immortals, but aimed to appeal to the person with less education. They were related to each other much more freely than the ones in the great family schools. Many of them came from the merchant class rather than the courts or the military, and they were looked down upon and despised by the

134 *Oriental fans*

feudal families; however, their work appealed to many.

Compositions

There are dozens and dozens of recognized rules and regulations from each period and what is fascinating is the interpretation put on them by the various schools of painting, some of them wrapped indissolubly with their philosophies. For instance, one school decreed that painting the Four Seasons with a scene of mountains should suggest in Spring 'joyousness', in Summer 'green moisture', in Autumn 'abundance', and in Winter 'drowsiness'. Then, in another example, the rules for painting bamboo: 'In fair weather the leaves should spread out joyously; when raining the leaves should hang down despondently; when windy they should cross each other confusedly and in the dew of early morning the leaves should all point up vigorously'. You can tell the various schools when they painted this subject by the way they interpreted the rules. For instance the Kanō artists painted bamboo leaves with their brush-strokes going upwards, the Shijō artists painted them with brush-strokes travelling downwards. Similarly, with scenes in snow the Kanō artists first painted the bottom of the snow-line and then by shading above, with very light inks, they produced an effect of accumulated snow. The Ōkyo School, a much more naturalistic school not so prominently in the mainstream of painting, managed a far more brilliant effect by using a single dextrous stroke of the well-watered brush, the point only of which was dipped in *sumi*.

There was an order for painting everything, which, once known, aids appreciation of the quality of the technique. Chrysanthemums, for instance, together with peonies, are begun at their central point, built up from within outwardly, the petals being added to increase the size as the flower opens.

In flower subjects generally the blossoms

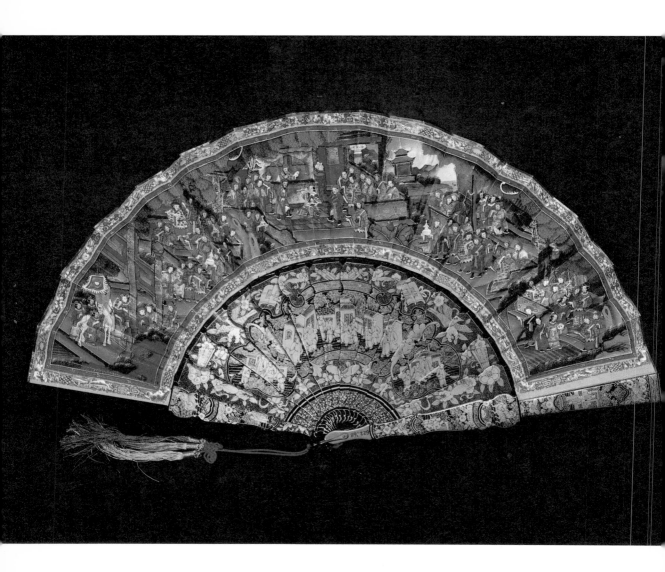

are painted first, then the buds, then the stem, the stalks, the leaves and their veinings and finally the dots.

The human figure is painted in this order: nose, eyebrows, eyes, mouth, ears, sides of face and hair, chin, forehead, head, neck, hands, feet and finally the clothed body.

The subjects which signify the various months of the year are of great interest; there are a good many for each month and a random choice is given here:

January: the sun rising above the waves
February: a cock and a hen with a budding
    plum-branch
March: the peach blossom
April: the wisteria flower
May: compositions with irises
June: scenes with waterfalls
July: the seven grasses of Autumn in various
    arrangements
August: rice-stacks with sparrows
September: chrysanthemums
October: geese flying across the moon at
    night
November: some of the gods of luck
December: snow-shelters of rice-straw
    protecting white chrysanthemums.

Two other fans from the Kanō school, figs. 92 and 93, show compositions which deal with a wish for long life; Jittoku with his broom is one of the gods of longevity (fig. 92) and cranes and pine-trees (fig. 93) are symbols of the same. It is again easy to see which is the earlier style of painting but at the same time one must remember that two quite differing techniques have been used. Fig. 92 is created in *sumi*, fig. 93 with pigments – techniques which are described on pages 142 and 143.

Beautiful, delicate embroidery is almost synonymous with the word 'China' and most world museums show some of their magnificent historic court robes. Fans in China during the eighteenth and nineteenth centuries were both painted and embroidered

and the symbols for the emperor or the people in his courts can always be immediately recognized on either.

Naturally the emperor had special symbols which were his exclusive right, whether embroidered or painted on a robe or a fan, these being all used at the same time: the sun, moon, constellation, mountains, dragon, flowery bird, temple cups, water weed, millet, fire, axe and the linear symbol of distinction. His relatives had similar robes with differing symbols according to their rank, and the eighteen high-ranking officials of the court had special motifs on their robes known as 'Mandarin' squares. These officials were divided into two camps, the civil officials and the military ones. The civil ones had all bird symbols, starting in order of rank with the white crane and going down to golden pheasant, peacock, wild goose, silver pheasant, Eastern egret, mandarin duck, quail and paradise fly-catcher. The military officials were allocated nine animals, in order: unicorn, leopard, panther, tiger, black bear, mottled bear, tiger-cat, seal and rhinoceros, and in both cases the birds or animals were issued in order of seniority. Not only would the official have his symbol embroidered on his robes but either painted or embroidered on his fan as well, with possibly some Buddhist or Taoist symbol on the reverse. They were all instantly recognizable. In China the artists added their signatures to their work rather prominently, often accompanied by a phrase such as 'In a dream last night I witnessed the scene I here attempt to produce'; in Japan the artist made his signature as inconspicuous as possible, together with his seal. The artists of the Tosa, Fujiwara, Sumiyoshi and Kasuga schools wrote their signatures and then, above them, in square or round Chinese characters they added their office and rank; the Kanō School artists did not add their rank but put in their Buddhist titles. Sometimes the date preceded the signature, but they were never permitted to put their age unless the artist

90 *Painted fan leaf. Onaga-dori (small, long-tailed bird) and chrysanthemums. Japanese, Korin School. 17th-18th centuries. By courtesy of the Countess of Rosse, Messell Collection*

91 *Painted fan leaf, sparrow with grasshopper. Signed Kwaito, dated Kanobo-Hitsuji (probably corresponding with 1811) Japanese, Shijo School. By courtesy of the Countess of Rosse, Messell Collection*

Opposite
92 *Painted fan leaf. Jittoku with his broom. Japanese, Kano School, 17th-19th centuries. By courtesy of the Countess of Rosse, Messell Collection*

93 *Painted fan leaf showing cranes and pine-trees. Japanese, Kanō School, 17th-18th centuries. By courtesy of the Countess of Rosse, Messell Collection*

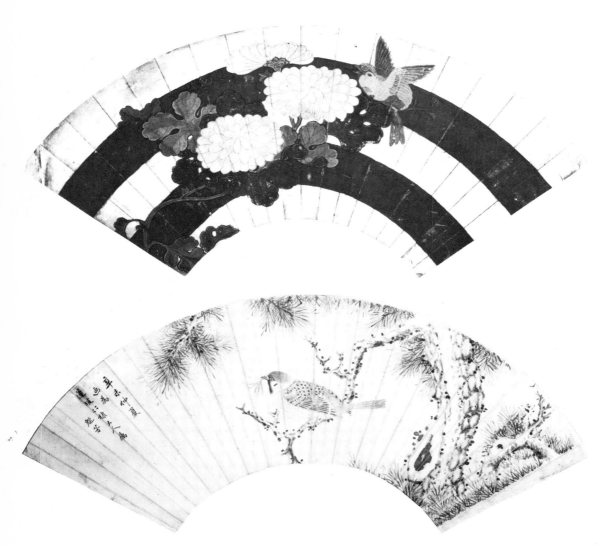

94 Fuji seen above the pine-trees. Colour print from wood-block. Ichiryusai Hiroshige (1797-1857). Victoria and Albert Museum, Crown copyright

was a brilliant child under the age of thirteen or a master over the age of sixty; and lady artists usually added 'Jo', which means 'woman'.

Oriental artists never felt it necessary to frame and glaze their paintings – they were either used as scrolls on the wall, or on the fans collected into albums, or (in Japan) on the hinged screens. Art was a part of life and living after all, scarcely to be hidden under glass and separated from people by slats of wood.

Decorating techniques

Painting originally developed in China from the art of calligraphy. This was always executed with a brush, and brushwork is the key to both Chinese and Japanese art, its heaviness and its lightness, the direction

95   Japanese wood-block
fan-print by Ando Hiroshige.
'Nishiku Ferry' from the series
Toto Katsushika Watashiba
Sukushi. Victoria and Albert
Museum, Crown copyright

of the sweep or the amount of paint or *sumi*
loaded upon it.

Until the fifteenth century the art of
painting in Japan was influenced by Chinese
teachings and much of the work was mono-
chromatic or in *sumi*: neither country used
oil-painting techniques, neither country ever
painted the nude; both of them used either
water-colours or their special technique of
sumi. They did not paint on canvas, but on

specially prepared paper or silk; they never
used easels but sat upon their heels and knees
with the paper spread in front of them protected from the flooring by some soft material.

Paper was an Oriental invention, made in
China in A.D. 605 and brought to Japan ten
years later. Japanese and Chinese paper of
the last five hundred years or more was made
from several different types of fibre: 'Bast';
Broussonetia papyrifera; *Edgworthia papy-*

rifera; *Morae*, the paper mulberry, and *Wickstroemia canescens*, which were mixed with paste, manufactured from rice, ground and boiled, and also from the roots of certain other plants as well as gum made from seaweeds. The tissue under the inner bark of these plants is soft, woolly and shiny, accounting for the lustre peculiar to fine paper, and the types mentioned above were especially used for fans as they were soft and reliable, not easily torn, light, durable and simple to paint or print upon.

One special type of paper fan used in the East is the water fan, made from the paper mentioned above which is then dipped in Rerilla oil and *shibu* juice, taken from the unripe fruit of the persimmon and extensively used for hardening purposes. The preparation is repeated several times, drying thoroughly between each application and a coat of colourless lacquer finishes it off, making it impervious to moisture. The natural colour of *shibu* juice is white but it turns to a deep reddish tint when exposed to the air and can be applied to any surface such as paper for fans or bamboo for frames; simple kitchen fans were made from paper and *shibu* juice without the extra expense of a top lacquer coat.

Crêpe-paper was used as well for fans, hand-made in shallow furrowed cardboard moulds and then decorated, and paper string was used too. To prepare the silk for painting it was first attached to a stretching frame with a boiled-rice glue, then sized with a mixture of alum and glue, taking care not to dampen the edges which would break loose from the frame. Artists from the Tosa school generally used a hand-made paper into whose composition egg-shells were crushed; artists of the Kanō school used either mulberry paper or the light straw-coloured rice-plant leaf paper, but they preferred on the whole to paint on silk and so did the artists from the Ōkyo school.

Japanese artists seldom outlined their painted work. Sometimes a rough sketch was placed underneath the silk as a guideline from which light charcoal markings (from willow-twigs) were made on the material, afterwards to be easily erased by brushing with a feather. The water-colours were mixed and the painting created after very long and deep reflection with light, rapid and delicate free-handed strokes – brushwork was paramount.

As brushes (called *fude*) were everything in the eyes of the artist, they gained in importance as the years went by and more and more attention was paid to them. Originally they were made in China of rabbit hair around which was wrapped the hair of deer or sheep, and had handles made from carved mulberry wood. After a time brushes were made of fox or rabbit hair with handles of carved ivory and were kept in gold and jewelled boxes or in pots of precious jade, covered in low-relief carvings. Officials in the Chinese governments were expected to write public documents with brushes having handles of red lacquer, and Ogishi, the greatest of the ancient Chinese writers, used for his brushes feelers from around the noses of rats and hairs taken from the beak of the kingfisher.

In Japan the brushes were made from the hair of deer, badger, rabbit, sheep, squirrel and the wild horse, different brushes being used for different types of painting or different subjects. The most important and distinguishing feature of Oriental painting was the strength or lightness of the brush-strokes, achieved after years and years of practice.

The original and favoured type of paint was *sumi*. It is the exact opposite of ink, which is a fluid acid, in that it is a dry alkali. It is a solid, the recipes differing from artist to artist, country to country, but often made from the soot obtained from burning certain plants such as *juncus communis*, or bullrush, or *sessamen orientalis*, combined with glue made from boiled down deer-horn. This is moulded into a black cake which, drying thoroughly if kept in ashes, improves with age. In much of the best *sumi* crimson (made from the saffron plant) is added for the sheen and musk perfume is introduced for antiseptic purposes, or a little white pulverized oyster-shell added gives a deadening and dull effect.

In China the best *sumi* was made during the Ming dynasty, in Japan the best was made at Nara, near Kyoto.

In using the *sumi* the black cake is moistened and rubbed on a slab called *suzuri*, producing a thick semi-fluid. The very well-cleaned brush is dipped first into clean water, then into the *sumi* and used at once; the quality of the suzuri is most important because of its mineral character and its effect on the *sumi*. The most valuable stone was known as 'Tan Kei' and used to be found in the mountains of Fuka in China where the water which flows is traditionally blue, the stone itself being violet with gold streaks in it and tiny dots called 'birds' eyes'. It was not always obtainable so in Tibet they used black lacquered paper or bamboo, and in Japan a rather similar stone which was found near Hiroshima. The use of pigments in the East is of interest when used on ancient fans (there are many to study in museums and especially historic ones in the Temple at Kyoto). Their blue is the natural lapis lazuli; white is levigated oyster shells; the basis of the reds is vermilion and oxides of iron; the greens are native carbonates of copper. The beautiful dark purple so often fixed as a dye is one of the most prominent in their catalogue of colours, made from a species of knot-grass. Over the years, only the blues, reds, whites and gold have proved permanent, the greens have become almost brown along with the silken leaf.

Printed fans

Many Westerners think of Japanese art as 'prints', but the Japanese themselves do not care for prints. They consider them lifeless reproductions, but, naturally, very useful to draw Japanese art to the attention of the rest of the world.

They dislike them for several reasons, partly because cheaper colours are used in prints, partly because more than one engraver could be employed (they claimed 'specialities' and preferred to work on faces or dress and so on), partly because the original old woodblocks are so worn out that they give badly blurred outlines, but mainly they disliked prints because the subjects were so plebian. A print was cheap so it had to appeal to a large market, and that meant it had to be understood by everyone, not just the scholars or connoisseurs, and 'higher thoughts' were too obscure for the lower intellects.

Yet, there are some great masters which are enjoyed by the Japanese and certainly many are collected voraciously by the Western World. It is worth looking out for the printed fan leaves of Suzuki Harunobu (1725-70), Kitagawa Utamaro (1753-1806) Katsushika Hokusai (1760-1849) and Ando Hiroshige (1797-1858). The Japanese like Utamaro because of his careful studies in graceful line-drawings. They admire Hiroshige for his landscapes. But they do not care too much for Hokusai because they think his pictures reflect too much of his restless spirit; his manner is too theatrical and exaggerated for their taste – yet they are happy he is appreciated elsewhere and especially in the famous auction houses of Europe and America. The old method of printing their designs differs slightly from that of Europe. The drawn picture is pasted onto a flat cherry-wood slab and then engraved. To reproduce it a layer of paper or silk is laid upon the block, weights are applied and great pressures. Various colours are then put on, with as many as twenty blocks altogether, making the printing of a colourful design an extremely tricky operation.

Once the fan leaf is finished it has to be fitted onto its sticks, generally very simple ones with printed fans, or left as a fixed fan. Sometimes perfume such as musk is put in between the leaves, but unless this is most carefully done it can easily damage or stain the fan. Sometimes, even after a hundred and fifty years, there is the faint but evocative drift of scent when wafting a Japanese fan. Figs. 94 and 95 show two wood-block prints, by Ichiryusai Hiroshige and by Ando Hiroshige.

By the middle of the nineteenth century, as we have seen before, Japanese goods were flooding into Europe. The earlier ones were sent hopefully, to gauge European interest; just as soon as it was obvious which art objects would sell and which would not, the whole tone became subtly altered and coarsened as the Japanese geared their economy to mass-production and slightly changed their style and colouring to appeal more to the Europeans.

In the beginning the number of Europeans who were interested in fans from the Far East was quite small. Whilst the average lady from Bordeaux or Bath would be using lace or embroidered muslins or ostrich feathers the aesthete would be carrying a Japanese or Chinese example either bought in Paris or at Liberty's in London. They appealed to people of avant-garde tastes because they were so different (and a great change from the exported Chinese embroidered fans), also because they were made by hand rather than mass-produced, and they took endless trouble to try and find out what the designs or symbols actually meant. Fortunately there has always been such discipline in those two countries that, with a little time and trouble, they could be understood.

This is the time, when mass-production started, that such connoisseurs as Leonard Messel began to make collections so as to preserve the hand-made fans. This collection, now the property of the Countess of Rosse, is one of the finest in the world, and includes some really beautiful and unique examples of both Chinese and Japanese fans. For a long time Oriental art has been underrated and misunderstood but the scholarly research and critical analysis carried out by collectors like these make the collection of Oriental fans, embroidered, painted or printed, feasible and enjoyable.

Feather, brisé and textile fans

Feather fans

In spite of their great delicacy, problems of storage and obvious ability to disintegrate, feathers have been used for fans since the beginning of time. They have been valued for their rarity, their colours and their individual qualities as decoration. No attractive or unusual feather has escaped, from the hummingbird feather mosaics of Mexico and Peru to the turkey and goose-feather fans of America, the woodcock of Scotland, the ostrich of South Africa, the peacocks of India and the Argus pheasant feathers of Borneo. Some are used in brisé form, some have to have a mount, some are satin-tipped and fronded with maribou but all of them intrigue.

Feather fans were the ones used by Oriental emperors of long ago. An ancient tale relates how the Emperor Kao-Tsong of the Chang dynasty (1326-1266 B.C.), having heard the cry of the pheasant, an omen of the greatest possible good luck, vowed that from then on he would only ever use the tail-feathers of that bird for his fans. Later the emperors of the Yuën and Ming dynasties traditionally used half-elliptical fans made from the wing-feathers of the pheasant.

Fans of many other types of feathers were used in China, often in the form of seven long tail feathers of some exotic bird. As is often the case with early fans, they had religious significance, the fan being one of the attributes of Chung-li Chuan, one of the eight Taoist Immortals. The number seven has also particular cabbalistic meaning in Taoism. These seven feathers corresponded to the constellation of seven stars on the left of the moon, the Great Bear, the seat in the Taoist Heavens of their supreme deity Shang Ti, round whom all the other star gods continually circulate in homage.

A favourite type of feather, in both East and West, throughout history, has been the peacock. The flamboyant peacock, the symbol of refinement, splendour and luxury, is now domesticated, but the Argus pheasant, to which it is related, is the opposite, far from domesticated, secretive by nature and living in dense foliage in Borneo. When the mating season begins the Argus pheasant starts his courting by strutting round and round a small sandy part of the river bank and displaying the inner feathers of his wing which has 'eyes' set amongst the golden brown down. The natives of the area are more than aware how valued the feathers are and set about catching the Argus pheasant in the only way they know how: they search for the obvious sandy patches which have been prepared for the courting dance, then set slivers of bamboo, sharpened to needle-like splinters, at angles in the sand, partially hidden. The male bird is far too intent on his annual gymnastic display to notice the dangers and

96 *The Ambras feather fan,*
16th century. Ceremonial
Mexican fan. Cane, interwoven
with cotton threads, on a wooden
frame, covered with leather and
agave paper to which the feather
mosaic is glued. The concentric
rings are in primary colours, and
the fringe is of Quetzal feathers
from a rare Central American
bird (Pharomacrus mocinno).
Part of the Montezuma treasure
sent by Cortez to Charles V in
1524. Museum für Völkekunde,
Hofburg, Vienna

the razor-sharp slivers cut into his legs as he gyrates, quickly producing blood-poisoning, from which he dies. His feathers, which reach very high prices, are packed off to China, Japan and the Philippines where they make beautiful fans.

Hummingbird feather mosaics are very rare and, once seen, never to be forgotten. They were made in Peru and Mexico and the Amazon Basin and some examples of the Paracos culture (about 2000 years old) are still to be found in the Ica Museum, Lima. The most famous fan (now known as the 'Ambras' fan) in feather mosaics is now in the Museum für Völkekunde, Neue Hofburg, Vienna (fig. 96).

These feather mosaics were (and are, as conservationists in Mexico are encouraging the revival of the old crafts) a highly decorative form of art rivalling illuminated miniatures on vellum for delicacy. The hummingbird feathers have an iridescence and metallic brilliancy that resemble some Limoges enamels, and they entrance the imagination with their silky-smooth softness and velvety surface. The Empress Eugénie of France was passionately fond of humming-bird feathers and made them fashionable on fans again around 1860. The general back-grounds were a solid colour and the feathers were used to make a floral design, sometimes joined by the iridescent feathers of the African starling, and toned down by having quiet tortoiseshell sticks.

Red Indian tribes used the feathers of the golden eagle for every-day use for men. Other refinements included magpie feathers, those from the rose-coloured macaw, white ducks' quills and eiderdown. The handles of those fans were made from tanned deer-hide or white doe-skin and special cedar-wood boxes were made for the chief's ceremonial fans.

Goose feathers have been used in their time, together with turkey feathers by Red Indian tribes and also by the Shaker Community. These people were a celibate sect who lived in mixed communities, having seceded from the Quakers in Manchester, England, in 1747 (dying out in 1909) and named after the dancing movements which formed part of their religion. The Red Indian tribes used these feathers because they were readily available, the Shakers used them because they were plain. In both cases the full feather was employed, fixed by the quills and simply bound.

Feathers were normally applied to fixed fans, but sometimes to folding fans as well. There is an absolutely beautiful fan, probably Dutch, of about 1770 in the Metropolitan Museum of Art in New York, which shows Bacchus and Ariadne at the centre of three medallions. The gaps between each medallion are filled with a multitude of different real feathers.

A mass of inventive fans was made during the third quarter of the nineteenth century, many with feathers. The Empress Eugénie was not only charmed with hummingbird feathers as a mosaic but she also loved the type of fan shown in fig. 97, where there is a stuffed hummingbird in the centre of the fan.

In fig. 19 there is another example of a fan such as this, where the singer, Adelina Patti, in a froth of pink, twitches her candy-floss fan over her shoulder.

Another type current in the nineteenth century was to have each ivory stick mounted with a feather shape cut from silk, white or pastel-shaded, and then edged with a fringe of real fluffy maribou along the top edge. Fans of coloured feathers gradually gave way in the 1880s to the colourless varieties, especially ostrich feathers. After the advent of electric light the brilliant colours in textiles and dress died away and made room for the lovely soft shades, the green-blues, cloudy silver-greys, lavender-pinks and creamy whites of the Edwardian days. With the softly moulded dresses in gossamer textiles, making the ladies look like a breeze of floating butter-flies, white ostrich feather fans were carried, mounted on simple ivory, mother-of-pearl

or tortoiseshell sticks. Rich simplicity was the keynote, and brightly coloured fans with plenty of gilding on the heavily carved sticks would have looked totally out of place with such well-bred dresses such as these.

Ostrich feather fans have a strip-tease connotation which would have mightily surprised both Queen Elizabeth I, who had them imported at vast expense from Venice, and William III who had to pay £30 apiece for them to top his state bed in Hampton Court Palace.

It is the male ostrich which bears the fine white tail plumes (and a few on his diminutive wings), and the female has much smaller brown feathers. Both can be plucked without harming the bird. During the nineteenth century the milliners and fan-makers demanded so many that ostrich farming had to

be taken up on a commercial scale to meet the market, especially in South Africa. There is a record of one shipment in 1909 of twenty tons of ostrich feathers valued at over half a million dollars.

When ostrich feathers, white, black or brown, are used for fans they generally have simple sticks of tortoiseshell or mother-of-pearl, relying on the dramatic effect of the plumes to have sufficient impact on their own. Equally dramatic was the effect in the 1920s of carrying one single tall ostrich plume dyed to the colour of the dress.

At the last bewitching flicker of court ceremonials in England in the 1930s, splendid clothes were worn (and reported in detail) together with the jewels and accessories such as the huge ostrich feather fans. These were either used in their natural colours or carefully dyed to match or complement the whole ensemble. The scene at Buckingham Palace – some people can still remember this clearly – was brilliant with the whole hierarchy of society, court and the diplomatic world parading like multi-coloured peacocks, an amalgam of the drag of heirloom lace, the twinkle of diamonds and the armour of soft feather fans. Court reports, later bound in scarlet leather and tooled with gold, showed precisely what each person wore. It is interesting to note the fans:

'Lady Maud Carnegie: Dress of white georgette embroidered with white and silver beadwork. Train of white satin lined with georgette. White ostrich feather fan. Ornaments: a diamond tiara of Russian shape, diamond and sapphire necklace.

'Mrs R. T. Hanson of the United States Diplomatic Corps: Apple-green satin dress trimmed with diamanté. Train of green silk net embroidered with crystals. Shaded apricot-coloured feather fan.

'Lady Beale: gown of raven's-wing blue chiffon, hand-embroidered all over with bugle crystals to tone in a design of graduated rings. Train of the same shade of Baghera velvet, suspended from an embroidered chiffon yoke with two beaded tassels. Jewels and a matching ostrich-feather fan.'

They came in every colour of the rainbow, every elegant material, mousseline de soie, point d'Alençon lace, flame and gold floral brocades, gold tissue, silver chiffon, silver beads, diamanté fringes, trains and diamond tiaras – and for at least a third of the ladies, a full ostrich feather fan. Some were white, some others were dyed; emerald green, flame, palest pink, amber or combinations of colours of which black and white or black and pink were the favourite. They looked magnificent and those who were there could never forget the sight.

Left
97 *Three fans. Top French 1870-80 with lace mount. Right French brisé, late 18th or early 19th century. Left circular fan with pink and white feathers and an ivory handle, from Brazil, late 19th century. Victoria and Albert Museum, Crown copyright*

Overleaf
98 *Three European fans. Top ivory brisé, pierced, painted and gilt, possibly English c.1780-90. Centre brisé fan, pierced mother-of-pearl, gilt metal guards. c.1825-35. Bottom brisé, pierced and painted ivory, c.1800. Victoria and Albert Museum, Crown copyright*

99 *A French 'Assemblée' fan with a mother-of-pearl stud, Vernis Martin, c.1720. Victoria and Albert Museum, Crown copyright*

100 *A 'Musical Garden Party', French, Vernis Martin, c.1720. A brisé fan of very fine quality, especially in the arbour work. Victoria and Albert Museum, Crown copyright reserved*

By the end of the 1930s the fans were no longer in fashion. The fan started life as an object made of palm-leaves or feathers. Having done the rounds of every other type fans went out with feathers again.

Brisé and lacquered fans

Brisé fans were popular in Europe from the 1680s onwards but became the rage in the eighteenth century when Madame de Pompadour took them up, especially the types made of ivory, a material which fascinated her.

A brisé fan consists of a number of blades of any firm or solid material without any leaf or mount at all. These blades can be carved, painted or decorated in any way and then held together in two places, a pin or rivet at the head and towards the other end a ribbon running through and attached to each blade in turn. It looks as though the same length of ribbon runs through from one end to the other but this is an illusion – a single length is chopped into sections and sewn together. The ribbon is firmly attached to each blade in turn so that, when fully extended, none of the blades obscure those next to them.

Brisé fans, probably as a result of their lasting popularity, have enjoyed a high level of craftsmanship. They can be made of amber, bone, feathers, horn, ivory, lacquered woods or tortoiseshell, the most dramatic (and easiest to photograph) being of ivory. Three European brisé fans are illustrated in fig. 98, two of ivory and one of mother-of-pearl. These are all from the late eighteenth and early nineteenth centuries, and have the smallness one expects for the period, together with the 'crocket' look.

Quite often when people are speaking of ivory they call it 'delicate' and treat it as though the slightest shock might shatter it. Granted some fretted ivory can look like frozen lace and give the appearance of greatest fragility, but when one considers how many of the fans which remain today have ivory

101 Chinese fan of pleated paper, 18th century. There are cut-outs on alternate pleats filled with either net or mica and stained mother-of-pearl pasted here and there. The ivory guards are fretted with coloured paper pasted behind and, unlike European fans, the sticks are longer than the leaf and shaped to curve inwards and have a knob-like finial.

Chinese brisé fan, late 18th or early 19th century. The guards of fretted and carved ivory, the upper section having goose feathers with a brilliantly painted decoration of long-tailed birds and flowers. Trimmed with maribou, having three coloured silk tassels and a small ivory carving in the round acting as a netsuke. Victoria and Albert Museum, Crown copyright

102 A Chinese lacquer fan, the sticks gilded with Orientals in a landscape, the paper leaf painted on both sides with groups of figures, their faces painted on ivory. 19th century. By courtesy of Sotheby & Co.

103 A 19th century Chinese fan; the leaf painted with Orientals in a garden, their faces painted on ivory; the rich ivory sticks carved and pierced with similar scenes. By courtesy of Sotheby & Co.

sticks in good condition then it is apparent that ivory is one of the toughest substances produced by the animal kingdom. It is practically impossible to splinter or to crack it (think of the elephants levering great trees with their tusks) and if there should be a break it is the fault of the carver.

We generally associate ivory with elephants, but there are other types: walrus and hippo teeth, sperm-whales, cachalots, narwhals and mammoths. All of these can be used in any shade from white to dark brown, although white elephant ivory is the most attractive for fans. It can be distinguished from bone by its tiny yellow and white striations which run parallel to each other. Bone has very thin hair-lines easily distinguishable as they run for only two or three tenths of an inch at a time, and hippo ivory has no striations at all.

The Chinese perfected ivory carving. The fashion for it in the past was so overwhelming that eventually their own ivory elephants were completely annihilated and they had to send to India, Malaya and Siam for tusks. One very famous family of expert craftsmen worked for four generations and founded the famous Peking Imperial Ivory Works of the seventeenth century.

Once the ivory has been prepared for a fan, carved, pierced, or fretted (after 1850) with a jeweller's saw (fretsaws are hardly fine enough), it is cleaned with pumice and water – never a polish with a spirit base as this alters the tone – then rubbed and rubbed with a soft clean cloth, until a lasting polish is produced.

Some of the earliest European brisé fans were made from ivory sticks covered with a painting and then protected by a lustrous varnish (fig. 99). These are generally all lumped together today under the heading 'Vernis Martin', after the Martin family, which perfected lacquered painting (see Glossary). These Vernis Martin fans were made at the end of the seventeenth and the beginning of the eighteenth centuries, never

104   *Standing feather fan, late
17th century. The feather mounts
are glued to a net within a rigid
frame; handle of turned wood.
Reproduced by permission of*
Country Life *by courtesy of the
Countess of Rosse, Messell
Collection*

105   *French fan 1860-70.
Mount of lace; sticks and guards
of carved ivory, painted with
groups of figures. Made by
Alexandre of Paris. Victoria and
Albert Museum, Crown copyright*

106 Painted ivory brisé fan, English, late 18th century. Victoria and Albert Museum

107 Painted ivory brisé fan, English, c.1780. The paintings probably by Angelica Kaufmann showing vignettes of 'The Shepherdesses of the Alps' and 'Gualtherius and Griselda' in ovals. The very finely carved rectangular section shows a carved and pierced scene of Venus in a lion-drawn chariot accompanied by putti. By courtesy of Christies

during the Rococo period, were copied in the nineteenth century, and are much prized. As none of them were ever signed it is almost impossible to tell which is a genuine Vernis Martin production and which was made and lacquered by other great ébénistes elsewhere in Paris, or in Holland.

Each country in turn made them as they were very popular in their time. It is obvious when comparing them that some must have been created by very sophisticated cabinet-makers and furniture-varnishers and others by mere amateurs. When one looks at such a splendid example as fig. 100 there is little question about its quality and parentage.

The lacquering of articles began in China hundreds of years before the birth of Christ and has been used continuously as a protective and decorative covering for all manner of wooden articles to the present day. It has always been admired for its mirror-like lustre, its lightness, durability and colour. The Chinese maintained their supremacy in the art of lacquering until in the seventeenth century the Japanese overtook them; connoisseurs consider that the moister climate made their technique fractionally better and Japanese lacquer fans are generally quietly black with gold enrichment.

There are two distinct classes of workers in lacquer, one who prepares the object in plain lacquer and the other who beautifies it. First the object has to be most carefully prepared. Every crevice or vein in the wood is filled in with sea-weed paste, rubbed down and finally covered with very thin paper that must be made to stick very firmly to the wood or bamboo – the more attention that is paid at this point, the more perfect the finished article. The main object of this preparation is not only to have the smoothest surface but to exclude any possible resin or moisture exuding from the natural wood to the upper surface and coming into contact with the lacquer, which would eventually damage it irreparably.

The refined lacquer is then applied by

brushing onto the surface and allowed to dry very slowly in a damp room, then smoothed down with magnolia charcoal in order to arrive at a uniform surface, and another coating is put upon the first. Successive layers are brushed on, sometimes up to several hundred coats, making the resultant article very hard and durable, even resistant to heat and water. The Japanese were unsurpassed during the seventeenth century for the quality of their lacquering, when Soyetsu, Koma, Ritsuo and Kajikawa were the masters. In the nineteenth century one looks for Zeshin.

When Western craftsmen copied Oriental lacquer during the seventeenth and eighteenth centuries they used a different form of gum, mixing it with turpentine which resulted in a loss of gloss and fine hair-cracks.

Lacquer was used for the sticks of fans in both the Orient and in Europe, either plain, painted, raised, incised, inlaid, carved or encrusted. The design on the leaf would be duplicated on the sticks if it was not a brisé fan, and, as often as not, on the box in which the fan would eventually rest.

As well as the normal brisé fan there are two specialist fans of note in the same idiom, the puzzle fan and the broken fan. The puzzle fan is made from painted unperforated blades which open out in such a manner that only half of each decorated blade is revealed, showing a scene on either side. Manipulate it the other way, exhibiting the other half of each blade and two totally different scenes can be shown. Quite often in the East the fourth and most private scene is pornographic, beautifully painted and very funny.

The broken fan is another trick, again made from unperforated blades and featuring a brilliant arrangement of ribbons. Opened one way the fan is perfectly normal; opened the other way the fan seems to fall to pieces, blades and ribbons tumbling into disarray, shocking and intriguing the viewer in the type of joke the eighteenth century vastly appreciated.

108   French fan, c.1920.
The mount is of turquoise silk gauze with an application of a matching stained mother-of-pearl design outlined in silver sequins; the sticks and guards are in matching stained mother-of-pearl, a type never seen earlier than the 19th century.

English folding fan, c.1915.
The silk leaf is palmette-shaped with an asymmetrically placed oval medallion painted with a standing lady in the dress of the period. The ivory guard and sticks are slightly shaped and have a painted band to match the border. Victoria and Albert Museum, Crown copyright

Many a collector will find an ivory brisé fan of the late eighteenth and early nineteenth centuries, or even a fan with ivory sticks and guards, and be unable to tell whether it had been made in Europe or in China. Allowing for the dangers of generalization, it could be taken that in Europe it was extremely rare to have any carving on unpierced ivory; when it appears that the work was cut out of the solid, close examination generally reveals that the work has really been accomplished by fretting the outline, carving it up, then backing the result with a thin layer of ivory. In most cases there was no disguise about it and the backing was especially made of brightly coloured foil or gilt metal so as to show up the design. This was a much quicker and easier way of treating ivory, hence cheaper too.

In China, although the sticks were often pierced and carved, the guards were generally solid ivory with plenty of meticulous under-cutting, and the relief was obtained by removing the ground with little drills and miniature carving tools.

When the Chinese were *not* going to carve in the round they merely incised the outlines of a scene, whereas the French and English worked more like the traditional medallists that they were, with several layers of modelled relief and no undercutting at all. A great deal of the work was carried out in Dieppe, long famous for its ivory-carvers and -turners. In fig. 103 there is a fine example of a nineteenth-century Chinese fan. With its intricate carving and its Chinese figures painted on the leaf no-one could ever mistake this for ivory carved in Europe, whatever the leaf.

Compare this with figs. 106 and 107 and you can see the difference with the best work in Europe of the time. Both of these are English ivory brisé fans, beautifully

carved in the European style, and both with
added painted decorations of typical European
subjects.

At the turn of the century some of the fans
were tiny and brisé, opening out to half a
circle, some opening out to a full circle like
a cockade. In these cases handles extended
from the guards so that they could both be
held in the same hand.

They made a feature of the blades, turning
them into curious but significant shapes:
arrows, with the sharp points at the head and
the feathers round the edge and said to be
'Love's arrows'; a bat's wing; a series of
snakes (Cleopatra's asp wriggled and writhed
throughout the whole of the nineteenth
century in the decorative arts) an orchestra
of violin-shapes or even made to look like
spinning Catherine wheels.

Their decoration, whatever the material

111 Chinese brisé fan, ivory,
painted and pierced, made for the
Western market. First quarter of
the 18th century. Victoria and
Albert Museum, Crown
copyright

used, was generally of cut-steels, tiny Wedg-
wood medallions or piqué, often with
quizzing-glasses set in the handles.

This was also a time for tiny brisé fans of
pale-coloured woods, horn, mother-of-pearl
and silver filigree, generally looking like
copies of their ivory counterparts. Many had
edges that extended in straight points like
architectural crockets, but when the fans
regained their normal size the points disappeared and have never come back.

Many brisé fans were made in filigree work,
an art perfected in China and Japan. The
metallurgist in Japan is famed for his beautiful
works, especially in small items (see fig. 109).

From the seven important metals the master
metallurgist could harmonize colours as endless in their varieties as the seven notes of the

musical scale, and he would create these masterpieces for war-like implements such as swords, daggers and fans to give combat the honour and respect they considered were due. They damascened with gold, silver and bronze, they inlaid with precious stones as well; they made marvellously gossamer silver-gilt filigree, especially for fans, and then decorated them with opaque enamels or with the turquoise feathers of the kingfisher gummed on.

Their fans looked beautiful, yet, when one comes to think about it, a silver-gilt filigree fan is just about useless in providing a cooling breeze; yet when comfort took second place to beauty they were very much admired.

Textile fans

Textiles of various sorts have been used for making fans in the Middle and Far East since records began. In Europe they have been mainly used since the eighteenth century (with the usual exceptions).

China and Japan

Probably the best known of these is the 'Fan with a thousand faces', normally believed to have come from the East. Tradition has it that the price depended upon the amount of little ivory faces there were in the scene, and that these fans are genuine portraits of members of Chinese courts. These 'mandarin' or 'Canton' fans have leaves of highly coloured paper, sometimes even of a very fine, highly coloured silk brocade. The faces were of ivory applied onto the design, sometimes the hands were as well and they were certainly not, as a dealer once stated recently, made from the lengthy finger-nails of the mandarins! Very often the beautifully embroidered clothes of each person seen in the composition (every one of which was slightly different) would lift slightly to show the garments underneath.

However, these fans are not what they seem. It is now known that much of the embroidery on these 'Canton' fans was carried out in the Philippines, and that the elaborate sticks were carved in China and sometimes all the ingredients were then shipped to Paris where they were assembled.

Many an owner of a Chinese 'fan with a thousand faces' believes that the fan was made in different districts of China and then exported to Europe from the port of Canton. This is not so. No Chinese would dream of owning a fan with anonymous 'faces', tiny slivvers of ivory or even rice-paper painted with exactly the same features on each, even though their garments might differ. In fact, the majority of these fans were made in the environs of Canton itself purely because it was the only port open to Europeans at the time. These European traders were very closely controlled, watched and guarded and only permitted to speak to the Hong merchants about their wares and to see the small dock-side booths (to begin with) and later small factories where the goods were made.

Naturally the merchants would buy other export goods, porcelain, ivory and textiles as well as the fans, but they were all of a type the Chinese felt would appeal to the European rather than anything they would consider using themselves. Their own fans would be personal, hand-made and each for a different purpose or to show their social status. Even so the quality of some of these mandarin fans (see fig. 103) is quite exquisite. They make a splashy show of colour in the room, but could never make as much money in the salerooms as a far more simple Japanese painted fan of the same period.

Some embroidered fans for home consumption were made in Japan and China. The embroidery had a variety of stitches, from French knots which were known there as 'Peking stitch', to satin-stitch, couching and appliqué-work. The colours used in Canton embroidery were very bright; work from the Yunnan Province was generally black or very dark blue, much of it being carried out in satin- and split-stitches.

The Philippines

The Philippines are one of the few places left in the world where fans are still used a great deal, and visitors from there to London have been known to be bewildered that there are no shops selling modern fans. A great many shops stock them in those islands, both the cheap paper fans for everyday use and the beautiful traditional fans to use in the evening or for the dance. Fan-making is numbered amongst their traditional crafts, together with weaving and embroidery.

It is extremely difficult to distinguish fans made in the Philippines from those made in Spain, another country where fans are still in use. Although the islands finally gained their independence in 1946 these countries have been closely connected since Magellan discovered them in 1521 on his expedition around the world (it was as far as he got; the natives promptly killed him) and named them after Prince Philip of the Asturias, later King Philip II of Spain. From that time on the Spaniards ruled there, intermarried with some, taught them a new culture, allowed them to copy their dress and generally interlocked with the people. Labour was very cheap so the Filipinos were set to carving the sticks for fans and they favoured a curious form of a fine curved openwork rectangle which is easily identifiable. They also made cases which are tubular, made from carved, pierced or fretted ivory or rare woods, often carved in sections, and having Moorish motifs. Trade between the Philippines and Spain was brisk and labour was far cheaper in the Indies so fan-sticks were carved and fan leaves were embroidered out there and then assembled in Spain.

Later on painted Spanish fans travelled to the Philippines in return and finally during the latter half of the nineteenth century (and

112   Bayanihan National Ballet of the Philippines. Dance of the Filipino Princess. Courtesy Bayanihan Company

lasting healthily up to the present day) fans have been interchanged from one country to the other, mainly of brilliantly coloured textiles smothered with flashing sequins.

To this day lovely fans are used in the Philippines; the most delightful method of seeing their strangely mixed origins and histories is to attend a performance of their National Dance Company, the Bayanihan National Ballet, where enormous study and research had been gone into regarding the backgrounds for the sequences. The dances, so amazingly varied and beautifully colourful, are all different, gloriously costumed, startling and exciting, and one understands immediately why they have to have a doctor permanently in attendance (fig. 112).

European

As we have seen, at the end of the eighteenth century in Europe the fashions changed to accommodate the new political climate, and fans changed, too. No longer could women have huge spreading fans of painted vellum but instead carried small fans with mounts of white gauze, silk or net, embroidered with garlands or Neo-classical motifs such as classical urns, with gold threads and gold and silver braids, occasionally appliquéd with seed pearls. The sticks and guards were of ivory or stained horn inlaid with steels. Spangles were all the rage, appearing on everything and fans were often smothered with pierced and shaped varieties. They were the modest woman's answer to her richer predecessor's jewels. So much the rage were they that they were celebrated in song:

> Spangles from bonnets fall,
> Shine on the toques of all,
> Sparkle on bodices small,
> And on the headbands fine,
> And on great hats divine
> Are spangles!
>
> On collars black as night,
> On shoes of virgin white,
> Are spangles!
> Spangles on ribbons glow,
> And on big turbans, lo!
> Nothing is here below
> Made without spangles!

As the fashion for fans changed in colour and size, they became so small that they were called 'Lilliputians' or 'Imperceptibles' (fig. 169). The latter name owes its existence to a *Dictionary of Etiquette* written by a Madame de Genlis in 1808, who scathingly reported:

113 French Neo-classical, late 18th century. The silk mount is painted with vignettes and embroidered with sequins, the ivory sticks are pierced, carved and decorated with Chinoiserie scenes.

Left *brisé fan, pierced horn painted with flowers, possibly Dutch; early 19th century.*

Right *Chinese brisé lacquer fan, 19th century. The scene is brilliantly painted in gold-lacquer, the sticks of silver filigree, the guards enamelled.*

Left *fan, mother-of-pearl and sequins. English c.1820. The mount is of stiffened muslin trimmed with gilt and silver spangles. The sticks of mother-of-pearl with engraved gilt pattern and a small silver looking glass, together with gilt holding ring. The central sticks are longer than those at each side so that the fan, when extended, is approximately semi-oval in shape. Victoria and Albert Museum, Crown copyright*

Right *ivory fan, painted on one side with a festival of the gods, on the other with a landscape and figures; on both sides imitation Chinese ornament. Vernis Martin decoration. French, early 18th century. Length of guard 21 cm. (8¼ in.)*

'In the days when women yet blushed,
in the days when they desired to
dissimulate this embarrassment and
timidity, large fans were the fashion;
they were at once both a countenance and
a veil. Flirting their fans, women
concealed their faces; now they blush
little, fear not at all, have no care to hide
themselves, and carry in consequence
imperceptible fans.'

During the early years of the nineteenth
century the imperceptibles became so small
they almost disappeared—one fan (in the
Messell Collection) shrank to a mere two and
a half inches in size. They could almost be
confused with the children's fans which

114   A very fine and rare
17th century fan; the panels have
painted mica inserts decorated
with peacocks, busts and flowers;
the sticks are very early examples
of tortoiseshell. By courtesy of
Christies

Right
115   There are only three known
examples of European mica fans
still in existence. The illustration
shown above, another at the
Cluny Museum in Paris and this
one in the Messell Collection.
The leaf is of pleated vellum,
framing panels of mica; the
sticks are of ivory. 17th century.
By courtesy of the Countess of
Rosse, Messell Collection

had been made throughout the eighteenth century, mainly in Italy where children have never been as excluded from society as in other countries. The difference, however, is to be seen in the decoration. Children's fans were also made to teach and had alphabet letters painted or printed upon them, or figures from one to nine, whereas imperceptibles were adult fans deliberately cut down in size.

As the century progressed, when the heyday of the true painted fan was over, a huge variety of textiles came to be used for fans; velvets, silks, satins, crêpes, cotton or gauze, and they were either embroidered or else it was these that were painted upon.

Many a fan was embroidered at home for

there was a great surge of interest in embroidery as a whole. It was visually accomplished by a fashionable technique known as 'art needlework', defined in *The Dictionary of Needlework* of 1882 as: 'A name recently introduced as a general term for all descriptions of needlework that spring from the application of a knowledge of design and colouring, with skill in fitting and executing. It is either executed by the worker from his or her designs or the patterns are drawn by a skilled artist.'

Most of the work was a direct reaction from the heavy Berlin woolwork fashionable earlier. The colours were not nearly as bright as the gaudy wools; the stitch used was mostly crewel-stitch and conventionally stiff floral

scenes replaced the great burgeoning loops of exotic flowers of past fashions. The whole design theme was an adaptation of Japanese art with many a hand-screen embroidered with long-tailed birds, fat little ducks swimming in sketched-in streams with a hint of cherry-blossom in the background.

Ladies from every country became enormously interested in an embroidered look; antimacassars and tidies were furiously turned out by the dozen, curtains and portières, decorative wall-hangings, counterpanes, coverlets, mantel-borders and piano-fronts and every single piece of household linen which could support a stitch. Naturally embroidered fans were made at home too, many on imported muslins with decorative themes which betokened 'I prefer the married

state' showing ivy or honeysuckle, the trumpet-flowered convolvulus or shy wild roses.

Paintings on fabrics rely as much on patience as expertise. From 1883 onwards gauze fans again came into fashion, not covered with spangles but painted with delicate pastel shades and what appeared to be a form of free-hand technique. This was done by using a carefully traced drawing which had the outlines pricked with a fine needle, the tracing placed on the fabric and a piece of cotton-wool dipped in charcoal powder (if the material was light) or in chalk (if it was dark) passed lightly over the holes. The tracing was then removed and the line of tiny dots were followed with a fine brush dipped in Chinese white or a neutral tint and

*116 English fan, c.1800.
Mount of gauze with applied
pierced steel decorations; sticks
and guards of stained horn.
inlaid with steels. Victoria and
Albert Museum, Crown
copyright*

other colours added afterwards.

Silk, satin, crêpe or gauze were often painted in gouache, in which white paint, instead of water, is mixed to colours, in order to make them paler. The gouache colours were bought already prepared or in powder form and dissolved in a tiny splash of water with just enough gum arabic to make the colour adhere. The less paint that can be used the better, for heavy paint looks chalky and often peels off the fabric in scales.

Painting velvet is again slightly different. Firstly any dressing or filler has to be removed from the fabric by washing or dry-cleaning and then the velvet has to be smoothed by passing a warm iron over the back, and pinned firmly to a drawing-board over blotting paper. The outline of the design has to be drawn or traced on with a lead pencil and it is important to keep the brushes scrupulously clean and a separate brush for each colour. The paints are diluted to a creamy consistency, sometimes with lemon-juice. First the outlines are painted in, saturating the velvet with colour – sometimes for large areas the back of the velvet is dampened in advance so that the colours soak in; then the shadows are painted in and finally the highlights and finishing touches such as the veins in petals, etc. After this the leaf is treated in the normal way when making a fan, as long as sufficient time is allowed to dry out the work first, and it is even possible, in some cases, to iron the painted leaf first.

Net was much used during the early nineteenth century, some for fans, in black or white and covered with spangles (see fig. 169) and also to strengthen very light fabrics such as gauze or India muslin, or as an interlining in gold or silver. It is strong, normally invisible from the surface in this context, and is extremely versatile. It often seems a shame that the gold or silver net had to be hidden in this way for often it was more attractive than the fabric it strengthened.

Net and gauze gradually gave way to lace

117 French fan, 1850-70.
Bobbin-made black Chantilly lace.
Guards and sticks tortoiseshell.
Width 60cm. (24in.). Victoria
and Albert Museum, Crown
copyright

Overleaf
118 Lace fans in black and
white silk worked under
Mrs R. Vere O'Brien's
supervision, from designs by
Miss Perry, the School of Art,
Cork, Victoria and Albert
Museum, Crown copyright

119 Fan given to Queen Emma,
mother of Queen Wilhelmina, of
the Netherlands, as a gift of the
Dutch people living in Belgium,
c.1880. Made of Brussels lace,
sticks beautifully pierced and
carved and gilt mother-of-pearl.
It shows the arms of the
Netherlands and the motto of the
house of Orange. Rijksmuseum,
Amsterdam

120 Detail of Queen Emma's
fan, showing the central section
of the lace mount with the Arms
of the Netherlands and Waldeck
Pyrmont together with the motto
'Je maintiendrai'. Rijksmuseum,
Amsterdam

Feather, brisé and textile fans   175

176 *Feather, brisé and textile fans*

during the latter half of the nineteenth century (fig. 118). Lace from every country that prided itself on its manufacture has been used for fan mounts, from the finest Chantilly to that which came from the Presentation Convent in Youghal, County Cork, from 1847 (fig. 118). Some very large and beautiful lace mounts were made in the same manner as that followed by Japanese artists when they painted their fans: the lace-makers considered the shape of the fan when making the leaf, rather than making an oblong strip of lace and fitting it onto the sticks and turning in the edges. If a lace fan has been turned in, then this lace was not made for the fan sticks at all but has been a later replacement.

Lace for fans was in either white or black, and fig. 117 shows a delicate Chantilly bobbin-made black lace fan. During the nineties many a white or black lace fan would appear on the stage, covered in sequins and strengthened by gold or silver net.

Dozens of happy brides have hidden their blushes by white lace or satin fans, often showing a delicate painting of the bride wearing her lace bridal dress, with the actual lace appliquéd on the fan and matching exactly the dress she wore; favourites amongst

these laces were Brussels needle-point, Genoa lace, Duchesse and Valenciennes bobbin lace and especially the wide variety which came from Honiton in Devonshire. Queen Mary had one such fan for her coronation from the Worshipful Company of Fan Makers, made of Honiton lace, blonde tortoiseshell sticks and two diamond studs. The design showed a central cartouche with her crown and cypher, with shields showing the Arms of England, Scotland, Ireland and Wales, and all along the border wound roses, thistles and shamrocks.

Another fan of this type was given to Queen Emma of the Netherlands in about 1880, as a gift of the Dutch people living in Belgium (figs. 119 and 120).

A final example of a textile fan is in fig. 121 which is known as 'The Kessell Experiment Fan'. The embroidery on this was done by a sewing-machine. A motif was drawn with a brush in Indian ink by Mary Kessell and then interpreted for the decoration of the fan.

In conclusion the varieties of fans produced in the later part of the nineteenth century illustrates the gradual turning away from the Fine Arts to the crafts.

121 The Kessell Experiment fan. This shows sewing-machine embroidery using white thread on a black background; designs by Mary Kessell. Victoria and Albert Museum, Crown copyright

The language of the fan

During the seventeenth and eighteenth centuries women paid particular attention to the care of their hands. Well-cared-for and perfumed hands and well-formed toe- and finger-nails were just as much considered then as now, as one of the greatest charms of a beautiful woman. Perfumed gloves, which were used in England as early as the sixteenth century, were *de rigueur* for the woman of the world 200 years later. Nails were buffed and polished and treated to a whole pharmacy-worth of lotions and potions, marquise-shaped diamond rings were worn to enhance the length of a pretty finger and draw attention to it, and the universal use of a fan proved one of the finest ways of drawing attention to a well-manicured hand.

'At the theatre,' said Blondel in *The History of the Fan* 'nothing is more curious than the manipulation of these instruments, playing with the expressive grace which is a silent flirtation. Before the play begins, or during the intervals, every one talks in the midst of a confused noise resembling the buzzing of an immense swarm of flies. The curtain rises – all resume their places; the conversation ceases; the fans, everywhere waving in varied movement, gradually, one by one, are put down in regularity of time; they flutter in captivating cadence, suggesting in appearance a crowd of variegated butterflies, and charming the ear with their delightful "frou frou".'

Addison, in the *Spectator* of July 1711, gives instruction for the uses of this 'weapon' – for 'Women are armed with fans as Men with swords.' He goes on:

'There is an infinite variety of motion to be made use of in the flutter of a fan. There is the angry Flutter, the modest Flutter, the timorous Flutter, the confused Flutter, the merry Flutter, the amorous Flutter. Not to be tedious, there is scarce any emotion of the Mind which does not produce a similar agitation of the Fan; inasmuch if I only see the Fan of a disciplined Lady I know very well if she laughs, frowns or blushes. I have seen a Fan so very angry that it would have been dangerous for the absent lover who provoked it to come within the wind of it. And at other times so very languishing that I have been glad for the Lady's sake that the Lover was at sufficient distance from it. I need not add that the Fan is either a Prude or a Coquette according to the nature of the person who bears it.'

According to Uzanne in *The Fan*, at the end of the eighteenth century there was a report in the *Spectator* of a lady who 'established in

London an Academy for the training up of young women of all conditions in the exercise of the Fan'.

'This exercise was divided into six portions, and the strange petticoated battalions, ranged in order of battle, were put through their facings twice a day, and taught to obey the following words of command: ''Handle your Fans'', ''Unfurl your Fans'', ''Discharge your Fans'', ''Ground your Fans'', ''Recover your Fans'', ''Flutter your Fans''. The fluttering of the Fan was, it appears, the masterpiece of the whole exercise, and the most difficult to be acquired by these singular companies of Riflemen of the Fan.

'Therefore the Colonel-Instructress, who directed the operations with a large Marlborough Fan, composed in favour of her scholars a small treatise, very clear and succinct, in which she concentrated all the ''Art of Love'' of Ovid; this theory had for its title ''The Passions of the Fan'', and tended to make of that flirting implement the most dangerous weapon in the war of Love.

'The same ingenious instructress had also established, at particular hours, a special course for men, with the view of teaching young gentlemen the whole art of gallanting a Fan, according to rules which guaranteed success after thirty or forty lessons.'

Clearly, the comparison of a lady and her fan and an armed warrior was one that lasted. Disraeli once said, 'A Spanish lady with her fan might shame the tactics of a troop of horse. Now she unfolds it with a slow pomp and conscious elegance of the bird of Juno; now she flutters it with all the langour of a listless beauty, now with all the liveliness of a vivacious one. Women are armed with fans as men with swords—and sometimes do more executions with them.'

Elegant men in the seventeenth and eighteenth centuries adopted the refined language of fans, twirling them with panache. Early in the eighteenth century it was said that there were three sexes—men, women and Herveys, referring to Lord Hervey, who appeared to be sexually ambidextrous. He always carried a fan and was known behind hands as 'Lord Fanny'.

We are told that a gallant would spend as much time and trouble on his toilette as the ladies, to the extent that he was even willing to have a joint of his toe remove to improve the set of his shoe. He wore gold and silver lace on his coat and his waistcoat, costly lace ruffles and frills, carried a gold snuff-box (a winter one and a summer one) a be-ribboned cane and a glittering fan. In 1768 Bickersteth, a social commentator, wrote of this male fashion-plate, 'as a coxcomb and fop, who shrugs and takes snuff, and carries a muff, a minikin, finicking French powder-puff'.

During the Regency things got worse. A report in 1818 describes effeminate men: 'they have small round looking-glasses, with mother-of-pearl handles, before which they clean their teeth, curl their hair, blacken their eyebrows, trim their whiskers and adjust their cravats. They are not ashamed to show themselves in theatres and public promenades with large vellum or embroidered fans and besides this they are terribly perfumed.'

One can be sure that Beau Brummel never intended attention to cleanliness and sartorial details to go to quite this length. In the end Queen Victoria said that she preferred 'a manly man' and made it quite plain that she expected the men in her court to forego the fan and take up something rather more practical.

If you were going to be taught how to use your fan the instructions at the London school were most explicit:

'To prepare the Fan,' it was stated, 'is to take it shut, holding it carelessly between two fingers, but with ease and in a dignified manner. To unfurl the Fan, is to open it by degrees, again to shut it, and to make it assume coquettish undulations in the process. To discharge the Fan is to open it all at once, so as to make a little rustling noise, which attracts the attention of those absorbed young men who neglect to ogle you. To ground the Fan is to set it down, no matter where, while pretending to readjust a curl or a head-band, in order to display a white, plump arm, and slender rosy fingers. To recover one's Fan is to arm yourself with it anew, and to flutter it with feminine and irresistible evolutions. To flutter the Fan is to cool the face with it, or, indeed, to translate to him whom it may concern, your agitation, your modesty, your fear, your confusion, your sprightliness, your love.'

'Whatever the heat of the climate may be,' said Charles Blanc in his *Art dans la parure et le vêtement*, 'the fan is above all things an accessory of the toilet, a means or motive of gracious movements, under pretext of agitating the air for the sake of coolness. This mobile curtain answers in turn the duty of discovering that which it is wished to hide, and hiding that which it is wished to discover.'

In fact, the art of playing the fan cannot really be learnt. Either a woman has a natural grace which can be developed into a flair for gesturing with her fan, or she will always look awkward. As the height of flirtation was reached through the handling of the fan, one could tell at a glance the status of a woman by the way she used her fan. One could say 'Ah, here is a young girl very much in the market for a husband', with one, or 'This is a gay young widow, perhaps more interested in a little gentle dalliance', for another, and for a third, 'This poor creature with her languid flapping is an ageing spinster who has completely given up hope'.

In hot-blooded Spain, land of dark eyes and stolid but dutiful duennas, it was customary for the young of each sex to communicate without words, keeping and breaking the rules at one and the same time.

Books came out, originally in Spain but later across Europe, to teach a young lady how to make up whole sentences with merely the careful actions of her fan. The scope of the conversation was limited to one topic:

Placing the fan near the heart: 'You have won my love.'

Rest the shut fan on the right eye: 'When may I be allowed to see you?'

'At what hour?' was answered by the number of sticks shown.

Touching the unfolded fan in the act of waving: 'I always long to be near you.'

Threatening with the shut fun: 'Do not be so imprudent.'

To press the half-opened fan to the lips: 'You may kiss me.'

Clasping the hands under the open fan: 'Forgive me.'

To cover the left ear with the open fan: 'Do not betray our secret.'

To hide the eyes behind the open fan: 'I love you.'

To shut the full open fan very slowly: 'I promise to marry you.'

Drawing the fan across the eyes: 'I am sorry.'

Touching the tip of the fan with the finger: 'I wish to speak to you.'

Letting the fan rest on the right cheek: 'Yes.'

Letting the fan rest on the left cheek: 'No.'

To open and shut the fan several times: 'You are cruel.'

To drop the fan: 'We will be friends.'

To fan very slowly: 'I am married.'

To fan very quickly: 'I am engaged.'

To put the handle of the fan to the lips: 'Kiss me.'

To open the fan wide: 'Wait for me.'

To place the fan behind the head: 'Do not forget me.'

To do so with the little finger extended: 'Good-bye.'

Carrying the fan in the right hand and in

front of the face: 'Follow me.'

Carrying the fan in the left hand and in front of the face: 'I am desirous of your acquaintance.'

Placing the fan on the left ear: 'I wish to get rid of you.'

Drawing the fan across the forehead: 'You have changed.'

Twirling the fan in the left hand: 'We are watched.'

Twirling the fan in the right hand: 'I love another.'

Carrying the fan in the right hand: 'You are too willing.'

Carrying the fan, open, in the left hand: 'Come and talk to me.'

Drawing the fan through the hand: 'I hate you.'

Drawing the fan across the cheek: 'I love you.'

Presenting the fan shut: 'Do you love me?'

Silly questions, silly answers, perhaps, but they would be desperately important in some provincial town where the young might never converse privately, marriages were arranged and about the only excitement in life was a clandestine meeting, a hurried kiss, a furtive note.

Duvelleroy of Paris added some of the sentences to the list above, presenting small books with the acquisition of an expensive fan. Yet there was another method of conversing with a fan which was rather on the lines of a late Georgian Morse Code. *The Original Fanology or Ladies' Conversation Fan* was invented by Charles Francis Badini and published by William Cock in London in 1797. On it were directions as to how to carry on a silent conversation and details of the way the alphabet was to be divided into five divisions, leaving out the letter 'J'. A total of five signals could be given and they were:

1 Move fan with left hand to right arm.
2 Move fan with right hand to left arm.
3 Place the fan against the bosom.
4 Raise the fan to the mouth.
5 Raise the fan to the forehead.

At the end of each word the fan was fully displayed, meaning it was then finished and another word would begin.

It was a most long-winded method of communication needing enormous concentration. For example, in order to produce the word 'Dear', one first realizes that the letter *d* is in the first of the five divisions of the alphabet, so the fan was moved with the left hand to the right arm. Then as the letter *d* is the fourth letter of the division, so the fan was raised to the mouth. Then the letter *e*, still being in the first division, meant the fan was raised to the forehead as the fifth letter – and so it went on, but at least it could say exactly what you wished rather than following a set pattern of phrases.

The original Spanish instructions were by Fenella, then later a Frau Bartholomeus wrote a set of fifty instructions in German and finally Duvelleroy produced a shortened version. It was all very harmless and amusing in company, an acceptable method of flirtation.

Rather more dangerous was the lady who, when out walking, let her fan drop to the ground deliberately. As the Baronne de Chapt has said:

'It is not a matter of indifference, a fallen fan. Such a fall is ordinarily the result of reflection, intended as a test of the ardour and celerity of aspiring suitors. They run, they prostrate themselves, and he who picks up the fan first, and knows how stealthily to kiss the hand that takes it, carries off the victory. The lady is obliged for his promptitude, and it is then that the eyes, in sign of gratitude, speak louder even than the mouth. What a brilliant role is played by the fan when it is found at the end of an arm which gesticulates and salutes from the depth of a carriage or a garden. It says to him who understands it that she who holds it in her hand is in raptures at seeing him. That is not all.

When a woman wishes to procure a visit from a cavalier who she suspects is in love with her, she forgets her fan; and this ruse often succeeds, for either the fan is brought to her by the gallant himself, or it is sent to her with elegant verses, which accompany it, and almost always invite a reply.'

From the cooling of Cleopatra to the deviousness of Oscar Wildes' Lady Windermere, the fan can assume a thousand different fleeting moods and lives. In the hands of an expert the conversation of a fan can be quite scintillatingly brilliant.

Appendix one
The making of a folded fan

The fan itself

A fan appears relatively simple on the surface but there are a surprising amount of facets to its construction. Not only is a fan small but it is continually in motion. Not only is it artistically treated with painted designs or exquisite embroidery, but it is folded, flapped, tapped and treated with little respect in the heat of the moment.

The aim of the fan-maker was to make a fan appear as delicate as a butterfly's wing but as tough, in use, as crocodile's hide. This was no easy task; and, as with all small objects, the more time and trouble taken over its making, the more expensive it would be irrespective of the materials used. It is equally true that not many people would pay high prices for an object of little intrinsic value, however good the craftsmanship, so it was wiser, when taking considerable trouble, to use the rarer materials and so guarantee extra profit.

There are basically two types of fans, the fixed fan and the folding fan, and both have been used all over the world although the folding fan is generally slightly more popular. Of these two basic types of fixed fans, one is Japanese and one Chinese, but neither exclusively so.

Japanese fixed fans

A length of about eighteen inches of bamboo is cut and prepared for use. Nine inches is then split down to the node or joint, which prevents further splitting. As the grain of bamboo runs perfectly straight it is then possible for fifty or sixty segments of the upper half to be obtained by careful division into exactly the same thickness. In order to keep these in position a diminutive bow of thick bamboo is then inserted just below the joint, the segments are deftly arranged crossways and a two-stranded string is interlaced alternatively between them, then fastened securely, steadying the framework by tension. Though the handle is generally formed by the bamboo left below the joint other substitutes are sometimes used which are either left plain or embellished. The bamboo segments are then trimmed to shape and a leaf applied and then decorated.

Chinese fixed fans

These fans generally took the form of an oblong or violin-shaped solid frame with a covering of silk or paper stretched across it, transversed by a mid-rib which was prolonged downwards to form the handle. Early European fixed fans were basically on the same techniques (see figs. 78, 82 and 95).

The folding fan

The principle parts of a folding fan are the leaf

and the stick, with endless variations on this theme.

The stick of a fan consists of a number of blades (also called sticks) with the outermost ones called guards purely because that really was their function; they were ordinary blades made thicker and stronger, firstly to strengthen the fan when in use, secondly to act as protection to both the stick and the leaf when the fan was folded, the widest part of the guard corresponding with the width of the folded leaf. The leaf was either double or single, cut in the form of a segment of a circle and made from a vast variety of materials such as vellum, textiles, lace, etc.

There are four main operations in the making of a folded fan: the work on the leaf or mount; the work on the sticks and guards; the assembling of it altogether and the finishing touches. 'And,' as Charles Blanc once said, 'when this formidable weapon of coquetry is completed, it is enclosed in a case, like a well-tempered blade in its sheath.'

European folding fans are familiar to us from paintings and costume plays, yet unless one has actually handled quite a few it is impossible to realize how much they can differ, from a cockade fan to a feather-mosaic, a brisé to a cabriolet. Some are enormous and some are tiny: some can be a mere quarter of a circle, darting with sequins and almost folding into the palm of a hand; some can be majestic and heavy with intricately carved sticks and encrusted guards, splendid for making Grand Duchess entrances; and some can be opened into a complete circle with a hinged pivot and a quizzing-glass set in the handle.

As they became an essential part of every woman's wardrobe they were eventually made of cheaper materials such as paper, with cheaper forms of decoration such as printing. These were made as a form of factory production.

The paper they used was hand-made and expensive, its recipe partially a secret and always valuable until the early nineteenth century when newly invented machines made it plentiful and cheap. It was made basically from rags and was thin, tough and had a smooth surface. It was never altogether white even in the beginning and age has added a creamy look. Eighteenth-century fans are far tougher than nineteenth-century ones which quickly lost their flexibility and colour.

The leaf

In a factory a paper leaf was prepared in a large room with a fire, not for the comfort of the workers but to keep the room warm and dry. It was first cut into oblong sections, larger than the final leaf would be, and two sheets of paper were glued together with precision.

The glue

Glue, again a semi-secret preparation, would be made of a revoltingly smelly mess of shreds of hide, skin and bones boiled down to a gelatinous mixture. The secret of its success would be in the softness of its consistency, its ability to stick firmly but with elasticity, allowing the two sheets to be separated at a later date so that the prepared sticks could be inserted. If the glue was too hard then the leaf would split, if it was too soft it would both ruin the decoration and possibly fall apart at the first gay flutter.

The hoops

Once stuck together the paper would be placed between two wooden hoops rather like small embroidery frames and stretched as tight as drums. Then the hoops, with the paper between, would be hung by small hooks to the rows of rafters so that the paper could dry in the warm air. When quite dry the paper would be separated from the hoops so that they might be used again immediately; the paper would be roughly trimmed with scissors and handed over to the decorator to paint the leaf with gouache, or to the printer to apply his printed design.

Factory personnel

Within a small factory it was natural that the decorator should be considered 'a cut above' the manipulator, and eighteenth-century prints of the trade show that the decorators were treated with far greater respect and comfort than the other workers. The more successful artists worked in their own studios at home but copyists in factories, generally women, worked deftly and quickly in the building. Each stage in the process of preparing the leaf or mount was assigned to different people and the same division of labour was allocated to the making of the sticks.

The sticks

Whatever the material chosen for the sticks, they had first to be roughly shaped and then shaved down to size in three gradations; proportionately thick at the rivet end, thinning down to the shoulder and thinnest within the leaf. The section of the stick inside the leaf is not on view so few people are aware how thin are the hidden blades; but the thickness of the leaf must always be taken into consideration, on either side of the blades, as the final leaf area must not be thicker than the stick.

The decorator of the leaf and the carver of the sticks had now to cooperate, for patterns of carved sticks in the better fans were either the same as the leaf or complementary to it. The sticks would then be engraved, fretted, pierced or hand-carved.

Sticks had always been made by hand until the invention of a machine in 1859 by Alphonse Baude of Sainte-Geneviève (Oise), an event which still had the authorities twittering fifty years later. At the same time a machine was invented for the pleating or folding of a leaf, and it made the preparation of a cheap fan so much easier. On the whole the same material is used throughout for the sticks of a fan, such as tortoiseshell or mother-of-pearl, but on occasion they have been mixed. One notable example was the Empress Eugénie's fan whose sticks were: two of white ivory, pierced and carved; two of silver filigree and enamel; two of ivory, pierced, carved and coloured scarlet; two of tortoiseshell, carved and pierced; two of engraved white pearl and two of gilt filigree enamel. It must have caught all the attention she desired.

Finally the sticks could be gilded, set with gemstones or encrusted; that is applied with a multitude of layers of gold leaf which gave an effect of solid metal. Either gold or silver leaf was used, sometimes together for contrast, sometimes left plain but more often burnished.

Folding the fan

Once the materials are ready and decorated the leaf must be folded or pleated and the sticks inserted. No-one was expected to pleat a fan leaf with the fingers. A mould was used (the best type was invented by the Petit family in France in 1760) made of walnut into which were cut twenty grooves radiating out from the same spot, each groove being about one eighth of an inch in breadth and depth. The worker or manipulator would gently push the leaf over the surface of the mould, trying it this way and that so that the principal figures or part of the painting never became hidden in a fold; when the craftsman or woman was satisfied he or she would press down the leaf onto the mould with a tool, a *jeton*, like a burnisher. Marking the folds had to be accurate as it was done once and once only, as mistakes could not be rectified.

When completed the folds were tightly pinched together to make them crisper. To prepare the leaf for the insertion of sticks the folds were carefully probed with a *sonde* (a tool like a narrow bevelled paper-knife about fourteen inches long) between the two glued leaves.

If the leaf was to be single the main decoration was made before mounting. The sticks were attached to the back of the pleated leaf with glue and a second painting over both the back and sticks was made later. The fan was then gathered together at the base. A rivet was inserted right through to hold the sticks firmly at the head and a decorative stud (gemstone, paste or mother-of-pearl) completed the operation. All the other trimmings were then added, ribbons, silk-floss tassels and knots, and loops after the beginning of the nineteenth century. The final touch of all was the addition of a tiny band of paper glued along the edge to hide the joined paper.

Fan cases

Fans in their original cases are infinitely more valuable. They can be made of wood, leather or lacquer or ivory. In Europe, until 1720, leather was coloured dark. Then fashion decreed it should be coloured red or green and after 1740 a very bright green shagreen was used.

Fan bags were made as well of flexible materials such as silks, satin, brocade or even of straw. Some were left plain, others embroidered; satin might have spangles or silken flowers, brocades might be quilted and woven straw enlivened with coloured beads. An effort would be made to harmonize bag to fan, occasionally using the same textiles and the draw-strings would match the ribbons or cords. A collector would be very fortunate to discover a fan case with silver mounts which have been hall-marked, dating the year of manufacture very accurately; after 1790 an exemption was made in England for these very small articles.

Good quality and expensive fan cases were lined with either satin or velvet and trimmed with matching gimp. Some original linings can be found in good condition for they had so little real wear. An expensive fan imported from the Far East would have its own matching lacquered box. Cheaper fans were brought over in large shipments and boxes were found to fit them in the shop where they were sold. These would not match the fan, and were made of paste-board covered with either pink or green paper, with the dealer's name stamped inside the lids instead of the maker's name.

Appendix two
Collecting fans

There is one golden rule about collecting fans, and that is to collect fans in good condition only. Never buy one if its quality is poor, if the fan needs mending or a stick is broken. There are hardly any people left in the world who can mend fans; more damage than good might come of mending them at home and professional attention might easily become a great deal more expensive than the original bill. After all, fans are only worth what a collector feels he or she can afford at a given moment. If he had paid a certain amount and it costs three times that to have it mended, would he have paid that total amount for a perfect fan in the beginning? Probably not. It is wiser to leave fans alone if they need attention because what you are paying for in a European fan is an amalgam of crafts-manship. The lure and fascination of fans is the way this craftsmanship is encompassed in a small space purely to delight; as they have said in the past about lace, 'It is nothing save a little thread descanted on by art and in-dustry', so it is with a fan – with grace, flair and style various crafts have come together and fused into enchantment.

It is as well to attend sales by the great auction houses if this is at all possible. Their experts take enormous trouble over the correct descriptions of fans, their prove-nance, their materials and even what a painted scene depicts. Should you go to a small firm to buy a fan then it is equally sensible to have the owner write out a written description of what he is selling you. It may easily differ from the label – and naturally, buying privately you have to use your own judgement and discount most family stories unless they have the original bill and description.

Then you have to examine the fan as a whole. The general balance is important: too much decoration on either sticks or leaf might end in disaster. Many a sequin-encrusted leaf has been so heavy that the netting has torn from the sticks and, equally, so bold an accent could have been placed on decorating the sticks that a vellum leaf has split under pressure. What is most important is balance and harmony.

Then one should examine the fan more carefully. First the leaf, to see whether it goes with the sticks or is a later replacement. If it looks rather thick then it might easily be a double leaf with a new one pasted over an old one. Look at the marks made by the folds. If there are cracks then it is not going to last much longer and has probably been kept in too warm a place. Secondly one should examine the painted decoration. Signatures, as we have seen, when prominently dis-played might quite easily be a Victorian addition; if a signature is put slanted amongst foliage or flowers, inconspicuously painted in the same colour, then it is possibly genuine – but still probably of the nineteenth century.

Printed leaves should have the name of the publisher somewhere, with the date of the Act (there were several after 1736), and almost all printed leaves are duplicated in the Schrieber Collection at the British Museum for you to check.

Lady Charlotte Schrieber is mentioned again and again amongst serious fan collectors. Cataloguers always include her name in their sales where relevant. Who was she? Apart from her title (she was the daughter of the Earl of Lindsey, born at Stamford) she was a scholar of some note. She married twice, first to Sir Josiah John Guest in 1833 and then twenty-two years later to Charles Schrieber M.P., living a splendidly full life of eighty-three years from 1812 to 1895.

Scholarship was highly valued in those days. Ladies were expected to do their best but not to overdo it, and, while their efforts to enter universities were frowned upon by the men, their cerebral ability at home was condescendingly approved. Lady Charlotte managed to do rather more than her bit. She is most famed for her translation (from 1838 to 1849) of the *Mabinogian*, which is a collection of ancient Welsh prose tales dealing with Celtic legends and mythology, literally 'instructions for young Bards'. For anyone who has attempted to learn Welsh, and Medieval Welsh at that, the mind quails at the concept, yet Lady Charlotte plodded on for eleven years and accomplished this Herculean task.

Fans must have come as a relief to her but she treated the subject with just the same scholarly approach. Having collected fan leaves as well as mounted fans from all over the world (on one page alone of the little notebooks she used are descriptions of fans from London, Paris, Antwerp, Berlin, Dresden, The Hague, Vienna, Augsburg and Gouda) Lady Charlotte finally bequeathed the whole collection, notebooks, catalogues and all to the British Museum. They are there today, but it must be stressed that they are not on view, though they can be seen if a written application is made beforehand.

Having decided upon your fan, where do you keep it? Some are bought already boxed and glazed, which can be placed in any room out of the direct sunlight and not above a radiator. Otherwise one must decide whether to display your fans in cabinets or to put them away – and putting them away is better. Wrapped in tissue paper and with two very light-weight rubber bands round both the sticks and the end with the folded leaf, your fans should lie in shallow drawers alongside each other and not on top of each other.

Heat and damp are the enemies of fans; heat dries them out too much and damp destroys the leaf or the textiles and the glue can become 'tacky'. So beware of a cupboard near a radiator. Fans which are sold in boxes are better than those without, but unfortunately many a dealer sells a fan in a box marked 'Duvelleroy' to a gullible customer, who immediately hopes that that famous firm made it. It comes as a sad disappointment to discover that they only made the box. After all, boxes were made to fit fans like shoe-boxes were made to fit shoes, the sizes do not vary all that much and they can be interchanged. However, if the fan comes with both box and bill, and the description tallies, then it is genuine.

There are no hard and fast rules about prices. You have to pay what a fan is worth to you. You pay vastly different prices for an orchid as for a daisy, but they are still both flowers; so it is with fans. You cannot use the materials again for anything else; it cannot be melted down. What you are paying for is your taste, for some rarity, and to fill a gap in your own collection. In the past fans were priced in shillings and pence if they were second-hand. Lady Charlotte Schrieber paid an average for hers of between three to five shillings, but in those days people looked upon 'old' things as belonging to the poor, and new things as the prerogative of the wealthy. Nowadays the reverse is true and antiques are very expensive. Even so, going to sales can be an eye-opener. Many a good fan changes hands at between twenty-five and fifty pounds (60 to 120 dollars), few go over two hundred; sometimes fans are sold in lots and you get several for the price of one. It is a safe way of buying them for then you are aware of what other people are prepared to pay. Buy fans for pleasure, not for gain. Unless you are very wealthy it is difficult to buy only eighteenth-century European fans which are painted, and it is better to try and make a varied collection with as many different types as you can find. It is also very interesting to collect from different countries, not just from Europe but from all over the world.

It would also be well worth your while to collect fans from China and Japan, painted, embroidered and printed; folding or fixed. Many people travel to the Far East nowadays and have the opportunity to poke about in the shops there, and an Oriental fan might easily become the centrepiece of your collection.

The last consideration is the insurance of your fans. They are worth insuring every time. First take a photograph of both sides of your fan and attach a description (which is duplicated for your insurance company) and put both photo and description in the bank. If the fan is stolen the photograph can help identify it; if it is never found then the insurance company will pay up if you keep the original bill.

Appendix three
List of people associated with the making and selling of fans

Denotes that this name is mentioned in the Schrieber Collection at the British Museum

*Agar. Engraver, eighteenth and nineteenth centuries

Alexandre, M. *Éventailliste*, Paris, nineteenth century

*Andre, Eugene. Signed lithographed fans, France, nineteenth century

*Angrand. Publisher, France, eighteenth and nineteenth centuries

Aparisi Sempere, Carmen, Valencia. Fan shop, contemporary

Arevalo, Cano de. Fan painter to the Queen of Spain, 1656-96

Armenteras, S.A. Barcelona. Fan shop, contemporary

*Ashton, Sarah. Publisher, England, *c.* 1792 onwards, five names for firm

*Ayoldi, M. Albiach, Valencia. Chromo-lithographer, nineteenth century

*Badini, Charles Francis. Publisher, London, designed 'Fanology' 1797

*Balster, Thomas. Publisher, admitted to Fan Makers' Company, 1777

Barber, Lorca y Cia, Valencia. Fan shop, contemporary

*Barlow. Engraver, England, eighteenth century

Barrington, Nash, E. Fan-painter, England, nineteenth century

Bastard. Engraver, France, nineteenth century

*Bartolozzi, F. Engraver, Italy and England, eighteenth and nineteenth centuries

Baude, Alphonse. Inventor of fan machines, France, nineteenth century

Bayalos, A. de. Designer for lithographed fans, Spain, nineteenth century

*Baylie, Ann. Fan maker, London, eighteenth century. Warehousewoman 'At the Fan and Sun at Chidley Court, near Carlton House, Pall Mall'

*Becquet. Engraver, Paris, eighteenth and nineteenth centuries

*Behrmann & Collmann. Publishers, London, nineteenth century

*Bell, John. Fan printed for especially, British Library, Strand, London, eighteenth century

*Bella, Stephano Della. Engraver, Italy, eighteenth century

Belleteste, Jean Antoine. Maker of ivory fan mounts, France, 1787-1832

Belli, Fra. Engraver, Italy, eighteenth century

*Belleville. Publisher, Rue Portefoin, Paris, eighteenth century

*Benizy. Designer and Engraver, France, eighteenth and nineteenth centuries

Berger. Engraver, France, nineteenth century

Bernal Ulecia, Francisco, Seville. Fan shop, contemporary

Bertarelli, A. About 50 fans signed by him in the Castello Sforzesco, Milan, eighteenth century

*Birman, A. P. Publisher and designer, London, eighteenth and nineteenth centuries

*Bisschop, Madame K. Painted Silver Wedding fan for Lady Charlotte Schrieber, 1880

Blay Jacinto, José. Valencia. Fan shop, contemporary

*Boitard, Louis Pierre. Artist, France, eighteenth century

Boquet. *Éventailliste* at the time of Louis XIV, Paris

Bonheur, Rosa. Artist, France, 1822-97

*Bonnart, N. Engraved hand-screen, eighteenth and nineteenth centuries

Bonneville. Engraver, France, nineteenth century

Bosselman. Publisher, nineteenth century

Boucher, François. 1703-70. Said to have painted many fans including the Bridal Fan for Marie Leczynska

*Boulard, C. Engraver, Rue St Martin, Paris, eighteenth and nineteenth centuries

Bourbier. Designed fans, some for Sarah Bernhardt, France, nineteenth centuries

Bôval, de Beck. Fournisseur, Brussels, nineteenth century

*Branche. Engraver, France, *c*. 1800.

Briseui. Carved ivory fan sticks for Alexandre, France, nineteenth century

*Bunbury, H. W. Designer of fans, English, nineteenth century

*Burney, Fanny. Known to have designed some fans, English, 1752-1840

Cahaigue. Painter in gouache, France, eighteenth century

Calamatta, Madame. Decorated fans, eighteenth and nineteenth centuries

*Callot, Jacques. Etcher, France, 1592-1635

*Cameroux. Fan sellers, Featherstone Street, Moorfields, London, eighteenth century

*Canaletto, Antonio. Venetian artist, painted some fans, 1697-1768

*Canu, Jean Dominique Etienne. Engraver, born Paris 1768

Carbonell Giménez, José, Valencia. Fan shop, contemporary

*Cardon. Engraver, London, eighteenth century

*Carracci, Augostino. Bologna, Italy. Etched designs for screens, 1557-1602

Carre, Mlle Alida. Fan-painter, Holland, eighteenth century

Chaplin, Charles. Painter, France, nineteenth century

Chapman. Fan decorator for Madame Rebours, Paris, nineteenth century

*Chassereau, Francis Senior. Fan-maker, England, eighteenth century

Chassereau, Francis Junior. Designer, England, eighteenth century

*Chaudet. Designed printed fans for Napoleon, France, eighteenth and nineteenth centuries

Chevalier. *Éventailliste*. Paris, at the time of Louis XV

*Chodowiecki, Daniel. Designer and engraver, eighteenth century

*Churton, Miss. Awarded prize at Exhibition in 1889, England

*Cipriani, Giovanni Battista R.A. Worked Italy and England, 1727-85

*Clarke & Co. Publishers, 26 The Strand, London, eighteenth century

*Clarke, Robert. Publisher and designer, London, eighteenth century

*Clarke, S. Designed printed fans, London, eighteenth century

*Clarke & Simmons. Publishers, London, late eighteenth century

*Clarkes of Ludgate Hill, London. Fan-makers, eighteenth century

*Cochin, Nicholas the Elder. Engraver, France

*Cock, J. Publisher, London, late eighteenth century

*Cock, J. & Co. Publishers, London, late eighteenth century

*Cock, John, and Crowder, J. P. Publishers, London, late eighteenth century

*Cock, William. Publisher, London, eighteenth and nineteenth centuries

*Colin. Painter, France, nineteenth century

Compte-Calix. Painter, France, nineteenth century

Conder, Charles. Painter, England, 1868-1909

Cooke, E. W. Designer, England, nineteenth century

*Cooper, Robert. Engraver, London, late eighteenth century

*Cooper, T. Engraver, England, eighteenth and nineteenth centuries

Corot. Publisher, France, nineteenth century

*Coustellier, Fernando Y Compia. Paris, fan-maker, nineteenth century

Couture. Painter, France, nineteenth century

Creaciones Doca, Valencia. Fan shop, contemporary

Dagly. Worker in lacquer, Versailles, early eighteenth century

Darley. Painter of flowers on fans, France, eighteenth century

Dausa, S.A. Barcelona. Fan shop, contemporary

Degournay. Printer, 22 rue Mazarin, Paris,

late eighteenth century

Delgado Soriano, Francisco, Barcelona. Fan shop, contemporary

Desameaux, Charles. Fan-maker, France, c. 1680

Desparcs, Claude Lectère. Fan-maker to Charles II, c. 1680

Diaz. Painter, nineteenth century

Doré, Gustav. Painter, France, nineteenth century

Dore, Madame. Painter on silk and gauze fans, France, nineteenth century

*Du Bouloz. Engraver, France, early nineteenth century

*Ducret, L. Publishers, France, eighteenth and nineteenth centuries

*Duncannon, Viscountess. Designed medallion fan, 1782, England

Duvelleroy, House of. Fan-makers and sellers, founded c. 1800 in the passage des Panoramas, Paris. Moved to 11 boulevard de la Madeleine, Paris, 1827. The London House opened 1849 at 167 Regent Street at the corner of New Burlington Street. In 1924 they moved to 121 New Bond Street, London, closing down finally in 1962. The firm received the English Royal Warrants from Queen Victoria to Queen Mary and won many awards

*Dyde & Scribe. Publishers, London, eighteenth and nineteenth centuries

*Egiarmon, Leonardo. Designer and painter, early eighteenth century

*Elizabeth, Princess. Drew designs for an engraved fan

*Elven, J. P. Engraver, England, nineteenth century

Espi Veres, Vicente, Valencia. Fan shop, contemporary

Essarts family, France. Workers in lacquers and varnishes, early eighteenth century

Estudios Tormo, Valencia. Fan shop, contemporary

Faber, John. Fan-painter, England, eighteenth century

*Fannière Frères. Carvers of ivory sticks for Alexandre of Paris, nineteenth century

Farge, Raymond le. Painter, France, c. 1680

Fayet, Messrs & Co. *Éventaillistes* for Louis XV and XVI, Paris

Feuchère, Jean. Engraver, France, nineteenth century

*Fleetwood, J. Designer of printed fans, 48 Fetter Lane, London, eighteenth and nineteenth centuries

Fleury, Robert. Painter, France, nineteenth century

Flummeren, de. Painter, St Gallens, Switzerland, eighteenth century

Folgado Sanchis, José, Valencia. Fan shop, contemporary

*Fontaine. Designer, France, early nineteenth century

Fossey, F. Decorator, France, late nineteenth century

Fragonard. Painter, France. Said to have painted Marie Antoinette's bridal fan, eighteenth century

Fraipont, E. Designed political fans, England, nineteenth century

Franco. Painter for Alexandre of Paris, nineteenth century

*Franks, H. Engraver, England, eighteenth century

*French, J. Publisher of Church fans, late eighteenth century

*Gamble, M. Publisher, early eighteenth century. 'At the Sign of the Golden Fan, St. Martin's Court, London'

*Ganné, J., 63 boulevard Menilmontant, Paris. Decorator, late eighteenth century

Garnier. Painter, France, nineteenth century

Garnison, Vve. Engraver, France, early nineteenth century

Gavarni. Painter, Italy, nineteenth century

Gérôme. Painter, France, nineteenth century

Germo, Leonardo. Painter, Rome, c. 1700

*Gilardini, Giovanni. Designed lithographed fans, Florence, nineteenth century

Giles, Miss. Winner of 1878 competition, England

Giménez Colomina, Luis, Valencia. Fan shop, contemporary

Giordano, Luca. Painter, Italy, seventeenth and eighteenth centuries

Girardin. Painter, France, nineteenth century

Glaize. Painter, France, nineteenth century

Gleeson, Robert. Gold Medal for carving sticks in 1878 competition

*Godefroy. Engraver, France, nineteenth century

*Goupy, José. Cabinet-painter to the Prince of Wales, 1736

Goya, Francisco. Painter on fans, Spain,

nineteenth century

*Granvilliers. Designer, France, early nineteenth century

Greenaway, Kate. Painter, England, 1846-1901

*Grignion, C. Engraver, France, c. 1761

Guerrero, Tomás, Barcelona. Fan shop, contemporary

*Guidicci, Angelo. Engraver, Italy, eighteenth and nineteenth centuries

Guillot, Jacques. Fan-maker to Louis XIV, c. 1680

*Hadwen, J. Publishers, London, eighteenth century

Hamon. Painter, used to work for Sèvres, France, nineteenth century

*Hammond. Designed and engraver, England, late eighteenth century

Hébert. Éventailliste at the time of Louis XV, Paris

Heine, Madame Charles. Painter, Paris, eighteenth century

*Herault. Made handscreen for the Dauphin's birthday, 1729

*Hermet, F. Designed lithographed fans, France, nineteenth century

*Herndley, William. Painter, Leicester Square, London, early eighteenth century

Hervy, G. Painter for Alexandre of Paris, nineteenth century

Hijos de R. Vives, Barcelona. Fan shop, contemporary

*Hincks, William. Engraver, England, late eighteenth century

Hiroshige. Painter and engraver, Japan, eighteenth and nineteenth centuries

*Hixon, Robert. Publisher, 6 Naked Boy Court, Ludgate Street, London, eighteenth century

Hofmann, Ludwig van. German fan-painter

*Hollis, M. Publisher, England, eighteenth century

*Holzer, I. Designer, eighteenth century

Honour. Fan-maker and Stationer, Fan and Crown, Long Acre, London, eighteenth century

*Hörman, Christoph. Designer, eighteenth and nineteenth centuries

Houghton, F. Winner in 1878 competition, London

Hylton, Richard. Publisher, England, early eighteenth century

Industrias Prior, S.A. Valencia. Fan shop, contemporary

Ingres, Jean Auguste Dominique. Painter, France, 1780-1867

Jacquemart. Painter, France, nineteenth century

James, Miss Charlotte J. Gold Medal Winner 1878 competition, London

*Jenner, J. Publisher, Strand, London, c. 1800

Jolivet. Painter, France, nineteenth century

*Jombert. Publisher, rue Dauphine, Paris, eighteenth century

*Jones, Charles. Publisher, England, late eighteenth century

Joucy, Jacques. Fan-maker to Louis XIII, seventeenth century

Juchau, L. J. Bronze Medal for 1878 competition, London

Kanō, Gano. Painter, Japan, eighteenth and nineteenth centuries

Kanō School of Painters, Japan

Kaufmann, Angelica R.A. Painter, England and Italy, 1741-1808

Kendall, Miss J. J. Winner in 1878 competition, London

Kerr, D. Publisher, London, eighteenth and nineteenth centuries

Kees, Ernest. Fournisseur, Paris, nineteenth century

Klagman. Engraver, France, nineteenth century

*Kleiner, S. Designer and engraver, Vienna, eighteenth century

Kokoschka, Oskar. Painter, England and Germany, twentieth century

Kymli. Painter of fans for the Elector Palatine, Germany, c. 1779

Lafage, Raymond de. Designer, France, eighteenth and nineteenth centuries

Lairesse, Gerard de. Painter, France, 1641-1711

Laird, Miss Elizabeth. Dublin. Won Gold Medal 1878 competition, London

Lami, Eugène. Painter, France, nineteenth century

*Laneret, Nicholas. Painter, France, specialized in marriage fans, 1690-1743

Laneret. Painter, France, eighteenth century

Langlois family. Specialists in lacquers and varnishes, France, seventeenth and eighteenth centuries

*Langlois, N. Engraver, France, eighteenth century

Lanoy. Engraver, France, nineteenth century

*Lasinio, Count Carl. Painter, Italy, late eighteenth century

*Laurent, J. y Cie. Publishers, Madrid and Paris, late nineteenth century

*Lauriere, J. Publisher, St James's St, London, eighteenth century

*La Vega, Fo. Painter, France, eighteenth century

*Lebeau. Painter and engraver, France, eighteenth century

Lebrun, Charles. Painter and designer, France, 1619-90

Legrand, Pierre. Fan-maker to the Duchesse d'Orléans, c. 1663

Leman, H. Decorator for Madame Lebours, Paris, nineteenth century

*Lemercier. Engraver, France, eighteenth and nineteenth centuries

*Lemercier, Bernard et Cie. Engravers, France, eighteenth and nineteenth centuries

Leroux et Cie. Fan-makers, 41 rue Notre Dame de Nazareth, Paris, nineteenth century

Lespiavt, Mesdames. *Éventailliste*, Paris, nineteenth century

Loch, Miss A. H. Winner in 1878 competition, London

Loire, Nicholas. Painter, 56 rue Dauphine, Paris, 1624-79

Louvion, J. P. Engraver, France, eighteenth century

Lucas, A. D. Winner 1878 competition, London

*Malbeste, Georges. Painter and engraver, France, early nineteenth century

*Mark, Quirin. Etcher on German fans, eighteenth and nineteenth centuries

*Marsay, L. G. de. Designer, 74 rue Faub-Poissonière, Paris, nineteenth century

*Martin, F. Publisher, England, late nineteenth century

*Martini, P. Engraver, England, eighteenth and nineteenth centuries

*Maurer, W. Designer, France, late eighteenth century

Meyer, Frédéric. France, fan-maker, nineteenth century

*Meyer, H. Painter and engraver, France, eighteenth and nineteenth centuries

Milner, M. 39 Cheapside, London, fan seller, eighteenth and nineteenth centuries

Minnigh, A. W. Fan-making firm Hague/Scheveningen, nineteenth century

*Moncornet, Balthasar. Publisher, France, eighteenth century

Moore, Miss M. Winner in 1878 competition, London

Moreau, Edouard. Painter for Alexandre of Paris, nineteenth century

Muller, Karl. German, worked in Paris, painting fans, nineteenth century

Nash, Edward. Winner 1878 competition, London

Navarro Monforte, Manuel, Valencia. Fan shop, contemporary

*Neele, S. T. Engraver, England, late eighteenth century

Nilson, I. E. Designer, England, eighteenth century

*Nixon, Robert. Publisher, 13 Bridges Street, Convent Garden, London. Published 'The Bill of Fare for a Wedding Dinner' fan, 9 December 1972

Okyo. Japan. Began the Shijo School of Painters

Onkruit, Theodore. Painter, La Haye, c. 1660

*Ovenden. Engraver, England, late eighteenth century

*Pagni e Bardi. Publishers, Via Maggia, Florence, eighteenth and nineteenth centuries

*Parr, N. Engraver, England, eighteenth century

Pascual, E. Valencia. Fan shop, contemporary

*Persier. Designer, France, early nineteenth century

*Peters, Rev. W. Designer of Chapel fans, England, late eighteenth century

Philippe. Painter, France, nineteenth century

Pichard. Designer, France, late eighteenth century

*Pichini, Cayetano. Painter of Spanish fans, early eighteenth century

*Picot, V. M. Publisher, France, late eighteenth century

Pinchbeck, Jonathan. Publisher and fan seller at 'The Fan and Crown in New Round Court in the Strand, London', eighteenth century

Pissarro, Camille. Painter, France, nineteenth century

Pitman, Miss J. R. Winner in 1878 competition, London

*Poggi, A. Publisher, Italy, late eighteenth century

Popelin, Claudius. Painter, France, late nineteenth century

*Preston, J. Publisher, England, eighteenth century

Prevost, A. Painter and *éventailliste*, Paris, mid-nineteenth century

*Rabiet, E. *Éventailliste*, Paris, nineteenth century

Race. *Éventailliste*, Paris, time of Louis XV

Radford, Miss Charlotte. Winner 1878 competition, London

Radford, Miss Emma. Winner 1878 competition, London

*Ramberg, P. Designer, England, eighteenth century

Rambert, C. Carver of fan sticks, France, nineteenth century

*Read, J. Publisher. England, 133 Pall Mall, London, late eighteenth century

Rebours, Madame. *Éventailliste*, Paris, nineteenth century

*Recouvreux. 37 rue Michel Lecomte, Paris. Lithographer, nineteenth century

*Renau, M. le Chevalier. Designer, France, eighteenth century

Riester. Engraver, France, nineteenth century

Rimmel. *Éventaillistes*, Paris, nineteenth century

Romanelli. Painter, Italy, eighteenth century

Rongeret. Worker in lacquer and varnishes, Paris, seventeenth and eighteenth centuries

Roqueplan, Camille. Painter for Alexandre of Paris, nineteenth century

Rousseau. Painter, France, nineteenth century

Roberts, John. 'At the Queen's Head in Holborn, near Hatton Garden, London, sells all sorts of Fine China Ware; the finest Hyson and Congo teas, Fine Double Flint Drinking Glasses etc & India Fans.' Eighteenth century

Rowley, the Hon. Hugh. Winner in 1878 competition, London

Rubio Valero, José, Seville. Fan shop, contemporary

Sayer, Robert. Publisher, England, mid-eighteenth century

Schwartz, S. C. Danish sculptor from Copenhagen, carved ivory fans, nineteenth century

*Setchel, J. F. Publisher, 23 King Street, Covent Garden, London, eighteenth century

Shannon. Designed lithographed fans, England, nineteenth century

Sheringham, George. Painter, England, 1884-1937

*Simpkins. Designer and engraver, London, eighteenth and nineteenth centuries

Skirrow, Mrs W. Winner 1878 competition, London

*Sloper, C. Publisher, Lambeth Road, London, eighteenth and nineteenth centuries

Soldé, A. Painter, France, nineteenth century

Soler Rocca, Gabriel. Valencia. Fan shop, contemporary

*Speren, G. Publisher, England, early eighteenth century

Spinetti, D. Painter, Italy, early eighteenth century

*Springsguth, S. Engraver, together with his son, eighteenth and nineteenth centuries

*Stagnati, Francesco. Painter, Italy, eighteenth centuries

*Stokes, Scott and Crosskey. Publishers, England, eighteenth and nineteenth centuries

*Stothard. Designer, England, late eighteenth century

*Strange, Sir Robert. Engraver, England, mid-eighteenth century

*Sudlow's Fan Warehouse. Publishers, London, late eighteenth century

Tárrega Folgado, Salomón, Valencia. Fan shop, contemporary

*Tellier. *Éventailliste*, Paris, c. 1729

Thesmar. Decorator of fans, eighteenth century

Theyer, F. Painter, Vienna, eighteenth century

*Thielcke, H. Engraver, England, eighteenth century

Tiquet. Designer, France, nineteenth century

*Tregellis, Miss. Kingsbridge, Devon, painted fans for Lady Charlotte Schrieber, late nineteenth century

*Tyssen-Amhurst, Miss Margaret. Winner in 1890 competition, London

*Unwins. Designer, France, eighteenth century

*Vagneur-Dupré. Designer, America, early nineteenth century

Vaillant. Engraver, France, nineteenth century

Vanier, Maison. *Éventailliste*, rue Caumartin,

Paris, nineteenth century

Vaughn, Édouard. *Éventailliste*, Paris, c. 1734

*Verazi, Julius. Engraver, Italy, eighteenth and nineteenth centuries

Vérité, Madame. *Éventailliste*, Paris, time of Louis XV

*Vertue, George. Engraver, England, early eighteenth century

Vibert. Painter, France, nineteenth century

Vidal. Painter for Alexandre of Paris, nineteenth century

*Visconty, Palamède de. Designer, France, eighteenth century

Voiret family. Pierre, Claude and Nicholas, painters, France, seventeenth century

Voorde, Aloys van de. *Éventailliste*, Paris, nineteenth century

*Watteau, Jean Antoine. Painter, France, 1684-1721

Wattier. Painter, France, 1800-1868

*Weightman, Thomas. Publisher, England, eighteenth and nineteenth centuries

*Wells, Lewis. Publisher and engraver at Gretna Green, late eighteenth century

Whistler, James McNeil. Painter, U.S.A., France and England, 1834-1903

West, Benjamin. Painter, England, 1738-1820

*Willaeys-Delaire, F. X. Painter and engraver, France, eighteenth and nineteenth centuries

*Williams, W. Designer, eighteenth and nineteenth centuries

Wilson, George. Designer, England, late eighteenth century

Winterthur. Painter, Switzerland, eighteenth century

Xanco, Barcelona. Fan shop, contemporary

Xavery, Francis. Designer, France, mid-eighteenth century

Zichy. Painter, Hungary and England, nineteenth century

Glossary

Advertising fans Fans have always been used for advertising purposes; inns, stores, hotels, airlines, drinks and luxury goods.

Akomé Ogi Early Far Eastern Court fans used from seventh century to *c.* 1860. They have thirty-eight blades of wood painted white and decorated with proscribed flower paintings on a ground of gold or silver powder, ornamented at the corners with arrangements of artificial flowers in silk, with twelve long streamers of different coloured silks, the rivet either a bird or butterfly.

Alum Indian ceremonial standard fan.

Alphabet fan With simple lessons for teaching children.

Asses skin Sometimes used for fan leaves; treated, perforated, painted and decorated with festoons of silver paillettes.

Assignat fan This refers to the decoration, often shown with the seven of diamonds, made *c.* 1791, pin-pointing the difficulties with paper money in France, at that time not worth one tenth its face value.

Battoir Sticks broadening out in a way which, in most typical examples, resembles a racquet.

Bridal fan An expensive gift from the groom to the bride, sometimes showing portraits of the bride and groom or their interlinked monograms. Simpler versions were given by the bride to her attendants.

Brin French term for the blades or inner sticks of a fan.

Brisé A fan with no leaf, made entirely from sticks which broaden towards the edge and are held in place by ribbons.

Cabriolet fan A fan which imitated a new two-wheeled vehicle introduced to Paris in 1755. The normal single leaf was divided into two (sometimes three) and decorated with painted scenes frequently featuring a cabriolet and its owner. The fewer, more simple sticks can be clearly seen like the spokes of the wheels.

Camaieu A painting on a fan leaf in different shades of the same colour, mostly rose or blue, popular in the eighteenth century.

Chapel fan Introduced for the use of Chapel-goers, *c.* 1796.

Chauri Indian fly-whisk.

Chicken-skin Skin taken from an unborn kid, dressed and treated for fans from the seventeenth century onwards. It has a very fine grain.

Children's fans Both children's fans and dolls' fans were seriously made, opening out to between 10 and 20 cms. (4 to 8 in.) when extended. Mainly made in Italy.

Church fans Printed ones were made in England during the eighteenth century. Used in the southern states of the U.S.A., often made of turkey feathers, placed in racks with hymnals and prayer books for the use of the parishioners.

Cockade fans A pleated fan opening out into a complete circle, the long guards form a long double handle.

Dagger fans These appear as ordinary folded fans but the handle withdraws and turns into a lethal dagger. Made in Japan (its importation into China was forbidden), and also in Italy as stilettos.

Découpé fan Made from vellum, rag-paper or silvered paper, cut out with tiny scissors to form an elaborate pattern on the lines of reticella lace. From the sixteenth to eighteenth centuries.

Domino fan Made with two cut-out sections for the eyes to look through, used as a mask, generally painted to look like velvet or lace.
Fan in other languages. Dutch: wanne. French: éventail. German: Facher. Italian: ventaglio. Latin: vannus. Polish: wachlarz. Spanish: abanico.
Ferrara fan Used by the ladies of Ferrara, looking like a duck's foot; the leaf opens to a quarter of a circle, formed of alternate strips of vellum and mica, delicately painted. The sticks of ivory with generally eight narrow blades.
Feuille, la French term for the mount or leaf of a fan.
Folding fans Invented by the Japanese, c. 668-71.
Gorge French term for the shoulder of the fan.
Gouache Method of painting in opaque colours consisting of a mixture of glue and water-colours, opacified by the addition of white or sometimes honey. Has the slight defect of drying several tones lighter than when wet. It is an elastic medium, giving a firm body, does not crack and its light tones are delicate and velvety.
Gumbai uchiwa Flat iron Japanese battle fans made from eleventh to twentieth century. The leaf was double, of leather and painted. The iron handle was about 40 cms. long (20 in.), painted, bound, and with a long cord and tassel.
Gun sen Folding iron Japanese battle fan, made between twelfth and twentieth centuries.
Handscreen A fixed fan introduced from China to Korea and Japan at the end of the sixth century.
Hi ogi Japanese court fans used from eleventh to twentieth century.
Jin sen Camp fan, from China to Japan, made from seventh century from pheasant or peacock feathers; handle generally lacquered, suspended from the girdle by a gold or silver chain.
Lorgnette fan Popularized by Madame du Barry, having a lorgnette inserted in the sticks or handle, but concealed.
Kanasawa fans These are special nineteenth-century fans made for a man, highly prized, created in the city of Kanasawa, west coast of Japan.
Kyoto fans These were etched, made in Kyoto where the art of copper-plate engraving was still largely practised during the whole nineteenth century.

Mai ogi Japanese dancing fans used between seventeenth and twentieth centuries, ten ribs.
Maki uchiwa Roll-up or revolving fan, flat, used in the East.
Mask fan A fan with a face painted upon it, eyes cut out, to use as a mask.
Mica A mineral of a foliated structure consisting of thin laminae or scales, dug from mines and found in volcanic areas. It can be used to decorate fans as small, almost transparent, panels. See fig. 115, one of the only three European-made mica fans known to be in existence.
 Mica was much used in the East.
Minuet fans Very small brisé fans of ivory, horn or mother-of-pearl made just after the year 1800.
Mita ogi A giant Japanese processional fan, about 2 m. long (6 to 7 ft.).
Monture, la French term of the stick of a fan.
Mosaique French term to describe sticks with a finely perforated ground and solid reserves carved in bas relief.
Mosquito fans Description in the *Demarest Monthly Magazine*, May 1880, U.S.A. 'Exquisite little affairs of the shape of the lily leaf, long tapering handle and beautiful decoration – silk of the finest sort – ivory, white, rose, blue, etc, worn at the belt and suspended by a chain. Intended to keep insects away.'
Mother-of-pearl Sensual material for the use of sticks. Three main types are Burgandine, poullette and black.
Oriental lacquer Refined gum from *Rhus vernicifera* or *Urushi-no-ki* tree. When cut the trees exude a resinous sap which turns black on exposure to the air. It is extracted during the summer months, allowed to dry, and ground into a powder and refined.
Panache French term for the guard-stick of a fan.
Panoramic fan Made in hexagonal form from stiff cardboard, the central scene can be rotated to show six other views by ivory-handled spindles. French, c. 1830.
Parasolette fan Large, circular fan with a central hinge so·it could fold away into a reticule. A nineteenth-century novelty.
People's fan Made around the time of the French Revolution in France from paper or wood, giving the affairs of the day, etc.
Piqué A form of decoration invented in Naples in the sixteenth century, spangling a rigid material in a permanent form. The surface of this

material is pierced with a tiny drill and minute gold or silver dots are inserted. Used a great deal on fans.

Punkah From 'pankh', a feather, a bird, also a generic term in India for fans, suggesting the beating of bird's wings to cool the air.

Rikiu ogi Japanese used in tea ceremonies. There are only three sticks and a paper mount and generally used as a tiny tray.

Ripidium Fixed religious fans, often in silver, still seen in the area of Greece.

Rivière French term for pin or rivet of a fan.

Sequins The word stems from the Venetian gold coin 'Zechino' first minted *c.* 1280. Sequins or spangles have been used to decorate since the seventeenth century in a variety of shapes and metals.

Sēsata Ceremonial standard fan from Ceylon (Sri Lanka).

Stick The skeleton or framework of a fan, consisting of the outer sticks or guards and the inner sticks or blades.

Straw-work Small pieces of firm straw are carefully cut down lengthwise and then applied to the material, bound in place with elaborate needlework or twisted threads. Straw was

originally adopted as the rallying sign of the Frondeurs and later used on fans.

Swans' skin Sometimes used for the leaf of a fan, one is in the Museum of Krakow, amongst a fine collection of fans.

Telescope fans A very popular type made in England, nineteenth century, so arranged that, when guided by a cord or tassel, it would telescope and become hidden in a tube.

Tête, la French term for the handle of the fan.

Vellum Fine calf-skin which has been carefully prepared and dressed, used from the sixteenth century for European fans.

Vernis Martin The Martin family of Paris perfected a European form of lacquered painting. There was the father, Étienne, and four sons. Their earliest fans date from 1709, the last from *c.* 1758. The painting is with oils, very thinly applied, delicately and highly finished. The entire surface was covered with colour, brilliant pigments flashing on a gold lacquer background, then coated with exceptionally fine colourless varnish. Their recipe was a secret.

Zephyrs Modesty screens of fans used by both sexes in Roman baths.

Bibliography

Aretz, Gertrude, *The Elegant Woman*, trans. James Laver. Harraps 1932

Arundel Society, *Fans of All Countries*, 1871

Blondel, M. S., *History of Fans*, Librairie Renouard, Paris 1875

Bordeilles, Pierre de, Seigneur de Brantôme, *Memoires des dames illustrées de France*

Bouchot, Henri, *L'Histoire par les éventails populaires*, two articles contributed to *Les Lettres et Les Arts*, Paris, January and July 1888

Bowie, Henry P., *On the Laws of Japanese Painting*, Paul Elder, San Francisco 1941

Catholic Encyclopedia, The, vol. 6, article on flabelli, Caxton, London and New York 1909-12

Chiba, Reiko, *Painted Fans of Japan: 15 Noh Drama Masterpieces*, Tuttle & Co, Rutland, Vermont and Tokyo, Japan 1962

Duvelleroy, *Exposition Universelle, Paris 1867* in *Rapports du Jury International*, vol. IV

Eitner, Lorenz E.A., *The Flabellum of Tournus*, College of Art Association of America, sponsored by the Archeological Institute of America 1941

Estoile, Pierre de l', *The Isle of the Hermaphrodites*, 1588

Flory, M.A., *A Book about Fans*, Macmillan, New York and London 1895

Fox-Davies, A. C., *Complete Guide to Heraldry*, Nelson, London and Edinburgh, revised 1935

Gibbs, Lewis, *The Diary of Fanny Burney*, Dent, London; Dutton, New York 1971

Gilchrist, James, *Anglican Church Plate*, The Connoisseur and Michael Joseph, London 1967

Gosson, Stephen, *Pleasant Quippes for Upstart Newfangled Gentlewomen*, 1596

Heath, Richard, *Politics in Dress*, in *Woman's World*, June 1889

Hughes, Therle, *Fans from the Leonard Messell Collection*, two articles in *Country Life*, June 1972

Ichitaro, Kondo, *Japanese Genre Painting*, trans. Roy Andrew Miller, Tuttle & Co, Rutland, Vermont and Tokyo, Japan 1961

Jenyns, Soane, *A Background to Chinese Painting*, London 1935

Motoi, Oi, *Instructions in Sumi Painting*, Tokyo 1958

Munsterberg, Hugo, *The Landscape Painting of China and Japan*, Tuttle & Co, Rutland, Vermont 1955

Noritake, Tsuda, *Ideals of Japanese Painting*, Tokyo 1958

Nuttall, Zelia, *Ancient Mexican Feather Work at the Columbian Historical Exposition at Madrid*, Peabody Museum of American Archeology and Ethnology, Cambridge, Mass 1892

Parr, Louisa, *The Fan*, article in *Harper's Magazine*, August 1889

Reig y Flores, Juan, *La Industria Abaniquera en Valencia*, Tipografia de Archivos, Madrid 1933

Rhead, G. Wooliscroft, *The History of the Fan*, Kegan, Paul, Trench, Trubner & Co, London 1910

Riley, Henry Thomas, *Memorials of London*

Robinson, Mabel, *Fans*, article in *The Woman's World*, January 1889

Salwey, C. M., *Fans of Japan*, Kegan, Paul, Trench, Tubner & Co, London 1894

Spielmann, Heinz, *Oskar Kokoschka: die Facher für Alma Mahler*, Verlag Hans Christians,

Hamburg, Germany 1969

Standen, Edith A., *Instruments for Agitating the Air*, Metropolitan Museum Bulletin, New York, March 1965

Uzanne, O., *The Fan*, J. C. Nimmo & Bain, London 1884

Van Briessen, Fritz, *The Way of the Brush*, Tuttle & Co, Rutland, Vermont and Tokyo,

Japan 1962

Waddell, Madeleine C., *The Rise and Fall of the Fan*, article in the *Antique Collector*, December 1966

Yee, Chiang, *The Chinese Eye*, London 1935

Yetts, W. P., *Symbolism in Chinese Art*, Leyden 1912

and the following catalogues:

Cust, Lionel, *Fan Leaves in the Lady Charlotte Schrieber Collection* Catalogue, British Museum 1893

El Abanico en España, Sociedad Española de Amigos del Arte, Madrid, June 1920

Fan Leaves, The Fan Guild of Boston 1961

Fan Makers' Exhibition 1878, London

Liverpool Arts Club Exhibition 1877

Redgrave, S., *Catalogue of the Loan Exhibition of Fans*, South Kensington Museum 1870

The Schrieber Manuscripts. 13 notebooks concerning the collection of Lady Charlotte Schrieber, British Museum

Catalogue of the Celebrated Collection of Fans of Mr Robert Walker – exhibited at the Fine Art Society's, 148 New Bond Street, London 1882

Index

Illustration numbers are given in italics

6.5.KL